KNIGHT-CAPRON LIBRARY
LYNCHBURG COLLEGE
LYNCHBURG, VIRGINIA 24501
WITHDRAWN

Douglas Blackburn

Twayne's World Authors Series
African Literature

Bernth Lindfors, Editor

The University of Texas at Austin

TWAS 719

KNIGHT-CAPRON LIBRARY
LYNCHBURG COLLEGE
LYNCHBURG, VIRGINIA 24501

DOUGLAS BLACKBURN
(1857–1929)
Photograph courtesy of
Dunbar Bros., Johannesburg (1897)

Douglas Blackburn

By Stephen Gray

Twayne Publishers • *Boston*

PR
6003
.L24
Z67
1984

Douglas Blackburn

Stephen Gray

Copyright © 1984 by G. K. Hall & Company
All Rights Reserved
Published by Twayne Publishers
A Division of G. K. Hall & Company
70 Lincoln Street
Boston, Massachusetts 02111

Book Production by Marne B. Sultz

Book Design by Barbara Anderson

Printed on permanent/durable acid-free
paper and bound in the United States of
America.

**Library of Congress Cataloging
in Publication Data**

Gray, Stephen, 1941–
  Douglas Blackburn.

  (Twayne's world authors series; TWAS 719)
  Bibliography: p. 152
  Includes index.
  1. Blackburn, Douglas, 1857–1929—Criticism
and interpretation. 2. South Africa in literature.
3. South African War, 1899–1902—Literature
and the war. I. Title. II. Series.
PR6003.L24Z67   1984   823   83-18582
ISBN 0–8057–6566–2

Contents

About the Author
Preface
Chronology

> *Chapter One*
> The Weapon of Ridicule   1
>
> *Chapter Two*
> The Adventure Antihero   40
>
> *Chapter Three*
> The Sarel Erasmus Satires   66
>
> *Chapter Four*
> Love and Labor: Last Statements   112
>
> *Chapter Five*
> Conclusion   142

Notes and References   145
Selected Bibliography   152
Index   155

About the Author

Stephen Gray was born in Cape Town, South Africa, in 1941. He took a masters degree in English at the University of Cambridge, England, and a masters in fine arts at the Writers' Workshop of the University of Iowa. Since then he has completed his doctoral study, published as *Southern African Literature: An Introduction.* He is professor and head of the department of English at the Rand Afrikaans University, Johannesburg.

He is the editor of many collections of South African writing, including *Modern South African Stories* and *Writers' Territory,* and has edited works by Sol T. Plaatje, Athol Fugard, C. Louis Leipoldt, and Herman Charles Bosman. He has published articles in journals in the United States, England, and South Africa.

He is also a writer, having published three novels—*Local Colour, Visible People,* and *Caltrop's Desire*—and some collections of poetry, including *Hottentot Venus and Other Poems.*

He is currently editing for publication the plays of Stephen Black, and working on a project of writing an alternative history of South African literature.

Preface

Douglas Blackburn's many achievements in the 1890s, and in the first decade of the twentieth century, as a British writer working in South Africa accorded him much fame in his day. By writers in South Africa he was hailed as the founder of their school of modern fiction. Of his seven remarkable novels, two in particular—*A Burgher Quixote* (1903) and *Leaven* (1908)—remain landmarks in the development of South African fiction. Today, Blackburn's reputation is in eclipse, and the period Blackburn dominated is not currently a popular one in academic studies. However, in order to understand the formation of modern South Africa, Blackburn is a crucial figure.

In South African studies Blackburn is out of favor for different reasons. A radical dissenter from the imperial sloganeering of his day, he functioned as an independent thinker with socialist sympathies, and as a lone commentator of extraordinarily controversial power on the issues of the black-white, British-Boer conflicts. As a journalist he launched many polemical, one-man newspapers, and his connection with South African affairs before, during, and after the South African War of 1899–1902 was immediate and uniquely insightful. His novels, arising out of this contentious period, reflect an involvement which is without equal in the issues which still divide the subcontinent. In many respects, Blackburn's views are still taboo in the country which he chronicled so thoroughly, and stirred with such satire.

This study uses primary material at all points, and, step by step, reconstructs the hitherto unknown connections between Blackburn's life, his writing, and his times. As almost all of Blackburn's creative works are currently out of print, I have not hesitated to quote from them lengthily, where this will assist the reader to acquire a feel for the flavor of the original. As Blackburn's career developed in haphazard sequence, I have grouped works by type rather than in order of first publication.

Blackburn's prolific amounts of journalism—some in prominent journals and newspapers, some irretrievable, most of it anonymous—have been referred to here only to illuminate points occurring in his fiction. In truth, his journalism, and his many factual works like *Thought-reading, Secret Service in South Africa,* and *The Martyr Nurse,* are of only secondary interest, and form a subject of their own—they receive only marginal attention here. A convenient, in fact, the only, sample of Blackburn's journalism is collected in *English in Africa,* in an issue which stresses his importance in the establishment of the press in South Africa.

This book is the first full-length study of Blackburn's life and work. It is also the first to unravel the facts from the myths that are perpetuated about him in works of reference. If much of what follows reads like a mystery story, that is because drastic corrective measures have had to be taken to sort the man out from the muddle of literary-historical records in South Africa. At times I have tried to dramatize some of the feeling of excitement when some information about Blackburn—an elusive man who intentionally wore many masks—came clear. At the start of this project I was not sure that a coherent personality would emerge; now I know that we have an important master on hand, the rediscovery of whom compels a reassessment of the history of the novel in South African literature, and which relates to many other social and political areas of South African studies.

To those who have assisted me in researching Blackburn I would like to record my gratitude: Dr. Trevor H. Hall of the Leeds Library, for letting me purchase the material on Blackburn he collected in preparing *The Strange Case of Edmund Gurney;* Mr. Eric Maskell of the *Tonbridge Free Press* for interview material; Mr. Rupert Croft-Cooke for interview material and for his written recollections of Blackburn; the Library of the Rand Afrikaans University, Johannesburg, for sponsoring the transcription of the Blackburn-Blackwood letters included in the *English in Africa* issue, and Mr. D. Fletcher of Blackwood's, Edinburgh, for making their archives available; the editors of *English in Africa,* Grahamstown, for publishing their Blackburn issue for the sake of posterity; and the National English Literary Museum, Grahamstown, which holds further Blackburn material.

Also to Mrs. K. J. H. Jeffreys, who first encouraged me to read Blackburn; Isa Gray, for searching the Society for Psychical Research records; Marianne Gray, for accompanying me on the Blackburn beat through Fleet Street and to Tonbridge, where we were the first

Preface

to honor his grave in many a decade; and Susan Gardner, for joining me at Loteni Valley to make final formulations.

Further acknowledgments go to the State Library, Pretoria, for the *Sentinel* material; the Strange Collection of the Johannesburg Public Library for the *Moon* and *Life* material; the Killie Campbell Library of the University of Natal for article and photographic material; and the South African Library, Cape Town, for review material. The British Library and Colindale Newspaper Library, London, furnished dates and supplementary information, and the Royal Commonwealth Society Library offered other assistance.

Finally, I would like to thank Professor Joseph E. Jones of the University of Texas, Austin, for initiating this project.

At the time of going to press a reprint of Blackburn's most central text, *A Burgher Quixote,* is planned by David Philip of Cape Town.

Stephen Gray

Chronology

1857 Douglas Blackburn born August 6 in London, son of George Blackburn, a journeyman leather-dresser, and Elizabeth Blackburn.

1880 October 22, becomes founding editor of the *Brightonian*, a weekly tabloid.

1881 *Disenchantment*, an operetta, with libretto by Blackburn and music by Henry Davey.

1883 June 2, *Angelo; or An Ideal Love*, an operetta with music by Jacques Greebe.

1884 May 17, the *Brightonian* closes under heavy libel claims. Writes the *Brighton Figaro*, of which no copies survive. *Thought-reading, or Modern Mysteries Explained*.

1886 Blackburn on Fleet Street, London, as reporter and theater critic for eight untraceable years.

1892 Arrives in South Africa. Works as journalist for the *Star*, Johannesburg, until 1895.

1894 Edits the *Moon*, a weekly pro-republican satirical newspaper in Johannesburg, and the *Moon Annuals* of 1893 and 1894.

1896 January, with Manfred Nathan, writes an anonymous pamphlet, "The Revolution—and After: Being the Secret History of a Failure" about the Jameson Raid of the previous Christmas. March 13, with William Ramsay Macnab, takes over the *Sentinel* in Krugersdorp. October, the *Sentinel* closed; name changes to the *Transvaal Sentinel*, which continues with the same editorial policy, "only more so."

1897 June 19, the *Transvaal Sentinel* publishes the pamphlet, "If There Should be War."

1898 March 30, the *Transvaal Sentinel* sold. Launches one-man satirical weekly, *Life: A Subtropical Journal*, in Johannesburg.

1899 Roving columnist for the *Standard and Diggers' News*, Johannesburg. April, *Prinsloo of Prinsloosdorp* by "Sarel Erasmus" published in London and Johannesburg by Dunbar Bros. and runs into three editions. October 9, Blackburn acts as a British correspondent behind the Boer lines, is deported, and by December is serving in the British ambulance corps and is wounded at the Boer War Battle of Colenso.

1900 *Kruger's Secret Service* published as by "One Who was in It." October, based in Pietermaritzburg, writes and collates *The Times of Natal* complete history of the war.

1902 Attached to the resident magistrate in Loteni Valley location, Natal. Convalesces and writes the first draft of *Leaven* and completes *A Burgher Quixote*. Contributes to *Man: A Monthly Journal of Anthropological Science*.

1903 *A Burgher Quixote*. Runs to two British and one colonial edition.

1904 *Richard Hartley, Prospector* published in serial form in *Blackwood's Magazine*. Returns briefly to Krugersdorp as part of Milner's repatriation of Boer War victims scheme.

1906 March-September, in London for medical treatment. Returns to Natal to resume detective work for the Criminal Investigation Department during the Bambata Rebellion.

1908 July, returns to England. August, prominent reviews in the *Bookman* and the *Spectator* of *Leaven: A Black and White Story*, published by Alston Rivers, with *I Came and Saw*, the final volume of the Sarel Erasmus trilogy. Rivers reissues *Prinsloo of Prinsloosdorp*, the fourth edition and the first to carry Blackburn's name. Contributes to the *New Age* on socialism in Africa, and a series of confessions to *John Bull* about his hoaxed occult experiments conducted with George Smith for the Society for Psychical Research in 1883.

1909 *The Detection of Forgery: A Practical Handbook* with Captain W. Waithman Caddell.

1911 As a response to the Union of South Africa in 1910, publishes with Cassell a joint "autobiography" with Caddell, *Secret Service in South Africa*.

1914 Free-lances for *Chambers's Journal* and other general magazines.

Chronology

1915 Last novel, *Love Muti*, set in Natal, dealing with the post–South African War period. Between Saturday, October 30, and the evening of Tuesday, November 2, writes a catchpenny biography, *The Martyr Nurse: The Life and Achievement of Edith Cavell*.

1916 Easter Monday, joins the *Tonbridge Free Press*, an independent weekly newspaper, as editor, and settles in Tonbridge, Kent. Contributes many urbane and witty articles to various newspapers, especially the *Daily Mail* of London.

1929 Dies of pneumonia on March 28 at the age of seventy-one in the Victoria Cottage Hospital, Tonbridge. Buried by his last wish without ceremony in a pauper's grave.

Chapter One
The Weapon of Ridicule
The Problem of his Identity

An account of Douglas Blackburn's life and work must of necessity untangle many a mystery, for he was a man who spun several mysteries about himself. Anyone trying to pick out the line of likely truths meets with dark corners and blind alleys, most of them set up by Blackburn himself. But the fact is that the real Douglas Blackburn—one of South Africa's greatest writers, and certainly the best of the many colonial Englishmen who wrote about life in South Africa at the turn of the century—has never been discovered before. This book is the first to attempt to present him, with some degree of accuracy, as he was.

The following biographical entry appeared in the *Anglo-African Who's Who* of 1905:

Douglas Blackburn of Loteni Valley, Fort Nottingham, Natal; eldest son of the Rev. Geo. Blackburn, was born in Aix, Savoy, August 6, 1857. He was educated at Wylde's King Edward Grammar School, Lowestoft, and read for the Bar. He has been connected with journalism since 1892, and is founder of *The Sentinel*, a progressive Boer journal, and has incidentally been engaged in numerous criminal and civil actions for libel brought by the Transvaal Government officials. He is the author of two books which have gained him a favourable notoriety, *Prinsloo of Prinsloosdorp* and *A Burgher Quixote* (Blackwood), and he has now in the press, *Richard Hartley, Prospector*. Mr. Blackburn has travelled considerably. He has written about sailing subjects, and has performed several unusually long single-handed voyages in small boats in British and Continental waters. Unmarried.[1]

This misleading and semifalse entry recurs unchanged—although Blackburn was alive and well, and certainly able to revise it—in the edition of the same *Who's Who* of 1907.[2]

Many subsequent reference works add details like the date of his death (1929) or of his later works (like *Leaven,* first published in 1908). Some rearrange the information somewhat, to accord with different views of Blackburn,[3] but, incredibly, none of them to date has taken the trouble to verify each and every detail, to test it against documentary evidence. If we were to read all the reference material that exists on Blackburn, we could not help spotting the rather shocking fact that information (or rather, misinformation) about him is seemingly endlessly recycled. To unravel his life, then, we need one basic tool: a healthy suspicion that wherever Blackburn went a tall story might have flowed unchecked, and that, as Blackburn himself enjoyed wielding the weapon of ridicule, his previous chroniclers might well have been deluded. Even a reliable modern writer like Rupert Croft-Cooke,[4] who knew Blackburn during his youth, and who has recorded his memories of the crusty old yarn-spinner in some detail, has been misled in his quest for the true Blackburn. The chronology of this book sets out the skeleton of Blackburn's life, and we may see at a glance how it differs from the *Who's Who* entries.

To start at the beginning: he was not one of many children. His father was anything but an English clergyman, in France for the birth of his son, Douglas. Although it is true that he was born on August 6, 1857, it is not true that he went to any renowned British grammar school of the time, and it is certainly not true that he studied law at a university. Then, not only was he "connected" with journalism, but he made it his entire livelihood, from a remarkably young age, and in a most particular way. By the date mentioned, 1892, he was thirty-five, and he had been in journalism since at least October 22, 1880, when, as a youthful editor of twenty-three, he issued the first number of his own independent weekly newspaper, the *Brightonian,* in Brighton, England. The "progressive Boer journal" that Blackburn edited (but was not the founder of)—the *Sentinel*—was by no means still alive by the time of the first *Who's Who* entry, and it was one of several similar precarious weekly newspapers that Blackburn had a hand in, or even wrote single-handedly. As a result, Blackburn was a great defendant in libel cases—in fact, the peculiar form of the libel cross-examination in court provided him with what might be called a literary genre all of his own, one that he used with great dexterity and all too frequently throughout his career. His *Prinsloo of Prinsloosdorp* (first published in 1899) might have been notorious in its own time, but was hailed as second only to the most enduring South African novel, Olive Schreiner's *The Story of an African Farm;* its ingenious sequel, *A Burgher Quixote,* ranks as the finest novel to have emerged from the Second Anglo-Boer War, or South African War, of 1899–1902.

Then again, Blackburn might well have traveled extensively in the realm of disarming raconteurism, around a bar-room counter, or in the thousands of columns of newsprint which he filled almost weekly throughout his long life, but the only evidence of transglobal expeditions that has turned up during the course of this research is of two voyages from London to Cape Town, South Africa, and back again, on regular commercial liners. He was certainly no pioneering solo yachtsman, like, for example, Joshua Slocum, who included South Africa on his round-the-world itinerary in 1897. The enterprising sailor mentioned in the *Who's Who* entry was quite another Blackburn, called George (no relation), whose biographical data seem to have become scrambled with those of our man. In all of Douglas Blackburn's fiction, there are very few scenes set at sea, the longest one involving a hapless landlubber being overwhelmingly sick on the brief passage from Cape Town to Robben Island.[5]

It seems that all that can be relied on with confidence is the fact that Blackburn was, indeed, unmarried. Although he was a popular best-man at several weddings, and a jovial host at seemingly endless celebrations of village baptisms and deaths, he did remain a bachelor to the end. Nevertheless, he was no misogynist; he wrote with deep sympathy and understanding of women.

Every other detail is up for validation.

Recovering a Personality

In researching this book, it was for the writer a constant source of perplexity as to why Douglas Blackburn's life and very extensive work could have been so uninvestigated and overlooked in the years since he published his last novel in 1915. Blackburn died too long ago for oral evidence from people who knew him to be plentiful. But in 1975 it was still just possible for a sleuth on the track of Blackburn to have the privilege of interviewing a man like Rupert Croft-Cooke. "He was so much an Edwardian writer," Croft-Cooke said, "and there were so many of them—E. M. Forster, D. H. Lawrence, Arnold Bennett, H. G. Wells—and even Rudyard Kipling, Joseph Conrad and Henry James were still prominent. No wonder poor Blackburn has been overlooked."[6] Blackburn's prose has much in common with the materialist style of the Edwardian novelists. It is understandable, perhaps, that a man who spent the sixteen middle years of his life—his brief period of creativity in fiction—out of the United Kingdom and away from the hub of Edwardian publishing should not have left any very noticeable mark in that period of busy activity.

Croft-Cooke also conveyed a key idea about Blackburn in his retirement when he described him as a "public raconteur interrelating fact and fiction, and no one in the small world of Tonbridge could tell which was which, probably." Croft-Cooke was able to describe precisely, across a gap of some forty-five years, the house in Ashburnham Road, in Tonbridge, Kent, where Blackburn lived his last years, the Rose and Crown pub in Tonbridge, which was his favorite haunt, and the adjacent offices of the *Tonbridge Free Press*, the weekly newspaper on which Blackburn worked from Easter, 1916, until his death at the age of seventy-one in 1929. With this kind of living testimony, it was possible to begin reassessing the Blackburn story from the tail end, in order to re-create a sense of the man and his world.

At first sight, his choosing the small town of Tonbridge for a last phase seemed strange. Tonbridge is set in fields of mustard and apples, hops and wheat, crowding behind hawthorn hedges a landscape noted for its oast houses, familiar to the railway passenger on route from London to the channel ports. The town itself to some extent explains Blackburn: despite its rural character, Tonbridge in the 1920s was a nexus both of waterway traffic on the low-lying canals that lead from inland to the River Thames, and an important crossroads and coaching stop between the sea at Dover and Hastings and the metropolis of London. Blackburn always liked to be at the intersection of all manner of human commerce and, far from being parochial, Tonbridge was a center of regional activity. As in Brighton (in the 1880s), in Krugersdorp (in the 1890s), and in Pietermaritzburg (in the 1900s), in Tonbridge Blackburn could keep his finger on the pulse of a town small enough to be encompassed by one reporter, yet large enough for country to meet town, old to meet new.

At 9 Ashburnham Road in June 1979, it was still possible to find the house in which Blackburn lived for his last decade and a half. There was no answer at the door, but enquiry up and down the street located an elderly couple who had moved in opposite Blackburn—believe it or not—in 1918. Although thoroughly sound of memory, they declined to reveal their identities. According to them, Blackburn lodged with a Mr. and Mrs. King and their daughter and son, and "very reserved people they were—only went out to church on Sundays, and had servants they kept on the other side of the road."[7]

This suggestion that Blackburn lived as a lodger in comfort in his old age did not quite accord with what the gravediggers of the Tonbridge Cemetery on Shipburne Road had to say. Blackburn lies buried there in a twenty-inch plot, number 32 of section B (entry no. 4234 of Saturday, March 30, 1929). "Yes, you could say it is definitely a pauper's grave"[8] was one sad conclusion. Blackburn was laid to rest by the Reverend J. Forster Holdsworth for £2 1s. 3d. on one of the coldest days Tonbridge had seen for a century. Doubtless, many of the greatest secrets about his life he took with him to his featureless, unmarked grave. Walking back from this doleful spot, this researcher followed Blackburn's daily route to work; it seemed typical of the Blackburn story that along the way back to the *Tonbridge Free Press* building in the center of town there were no less than six British pubs to be called in on within half a mile.

At least the *Tonbridge Free Press,* although now defunct, had not forgotten Douglas Blackburn. In their centenary publication the "famous Douglas Blackburn" is described as a most flamboyant character, and "author, mesmerist, spiritualist, one time magistrate in South Africa and a world-travelled man in many capacities."[9] The source of this information, Mr. Eric Maskell, who was one of the two juniors who ran the paper under "Blackie," recalled him clearly. Among many other reminiscences, he provided the following: "Oh yes, he was quite a character, a leg-puller. You couldn't always tell if he was serious in telling a story. . . . He was all for a bit of romance, but he was a man with a tremendous knowledge. But he was a rascal in his younger days. Do you know the story of when he ran off with an auctioneer's wife? In the Rose and Crown, which was next to our sub-office, he'd tell stories, he'd always start: 'When I was in South Africa and a magistrate. . . .' If a news story came in, he'd rush round and say he'd knock it out in ten minutes."[10]

Pressed for further recollections, Maskell came up with the following:

He was stocky, fairly broad and, say, 5' 9". And he was always in a hurry, and very bald with a few wisps of hair, sort of a Pickwickian figure. He wore dark clothing always, with a wing collar and a bow-tie. He disliked women intensely; I think he was afraid of them. Whenever one came into our two-part office, he'd slam his door and complain about blasted women again. He could have done with some looking after. I'll always remember him, though, taking his stroll around the castle wall. He smoked a lot, rolled his own, and his lapels always had ash down the front of them. Drink?—no, he didn't drink overmuch—he gave himself a 2/-allowance a day, for four or five pints of beer.

His weekly salary was a mere £3 10s., and a share of the profits of the newspaper, but, as Maskell remarked, there were never any profits, despite the fact that the *Tonbridge Free Press*'s circulation jumped from 2,500 to 4,000 during Blackburn's term as editor. Maskell concluded rather ruefully: "Ah, but Blackie was a reformed character, in his old days." It was clear from Croft-Cooke, Maskell, the neighbors, and the gravediggers that in Tonbridge Blackburn's memory was held in affectionate esteem.

Brighton Days

The next step in uncovering the story of Blackburn's life took an unfortunate, even unpleasant turn. It hinged on the tip that Blackburn had been a mesmerist or a spiritualist of some sort. Enquiries at the Society for Psychical Research in London drew forth some confusion between Douglas Blackburn and a wealthy contemporary, Charles Blackburn, who sponsored many investigations into psychic matters in the 1880s. Sorting the millionaire Blackburn out from the poor journalist took some trouble and also, incidentally, accounted for some further items of misinformation in the *Who's Who* entries.

The British Library has a copy of the correct Blackburn's first publication in book form, a 100-page work called *Thought-reading, or Modern Mysteries Explained,* which contains chapters on thought reading, occultism, mesmerism, etc., designed as a layman's key to the psychological puzzles of the day. We might feel that this is a bit far from the beginnings of a career of masterly fiction writing,

The Weapon of Ridicule

but *Thought-reading* is not merely a handbook on do-it-yourself hypnotism. It is also something of a work of literary criticism, and very typical of the correct Blackburn's style:

> No persons, familiar with popular literature, can have failed to remark how largely it has become permeated of late by the psychological element. The Occult, in some form, is seized upon with avidity by romancist and didactic writer alike. The psychological novel pure and simple has become a familiar institution, while those in which the mystical is introduced as a subsidiary feature are legion. The dark-eyed hero who exercises a strange, magnetic influence, malefic or otherwise, over the *spirituelle* heroine, has been cast for a leading part amongst the *dramatis personae* of the novelist; while the "mysterious psychic affinity" between the lovers is a condition as essential to the working out of the plot as the prime motive itself.[11]

Blackburn goes on to trace the development of mystical thought from the Mrs. Radcliffe school of Gothic mysteries of the 1790s through many works, including the hot sellers of the 1884 season, Lord Lytton's *Zanoni* and F. Marion Crawford's *Mr Isaacs*, the first theosophical novel. He also deals with witchcraft, shamanism, magic, and all forms of spirit mediumship as they had occurred in fiction. In his own novels he would frequently handle these matters in turn.

His extensive researches into this range of subjects were conducted in the British Museum Reading Room, to which in later life he would personally deposit copies of all his books, complete with inscriptions detailing the circumstances of their composition. *Thought-reading* is nothing like what its title would suggest. Nowhere in the text does Blackburn commit himself to any declaration of faith in, for example, the efficacy of extrasensory perception. Rather, it makes gentle and practical recommendations that will "materially assist [the reader] in grasping and appreciating the spirit of the psychic tendency of the day, and perhaps assist him in his attempts to discover for himself the key of the hidden mysteries of the Occult World" (*TR*, 11). The double meanings are there for those who read carefully enough, but this researcher remained convinced for the time being that Blackburn was a sincere early Spiritualist.

Then came the alarming discovery that many times Blackburn had been cast as a villain and a blackguard, notably by the very Society for Psychical Research for which he conducted many elaborate, carefully monitored experiments over the years 1883–84, with a younger partner named George Albert Smith.[12]

In 1881, Blackburn, aged twenty-four, while a correspondent on the *Sussex Post* in Brighton, became the founding editor of a polemical weekly newspaper, the *Brightonian*. This paper, a gossip-purveying scandal sheet, was, like its editor, of boiling spirit and volatile temperament. This is the period during which Blackburn allegedly abducted the auctioneer's wife, one Mrs. Parsons, and spent several nights with her in a London hotel—Blackburn was cited as the corespondent in the Old Bailey divorce case. This is also the period when he first landed in serious legal difficulties through libeling a crooked Brighton town councillor, with whom he fought a vendetta that sold many sensational issues of the *Brightonian*. The libel is in the form of a poem, one of no more than three by Blackburn that have been recovered during this research. The victim's name is not given in the poem, but his identity was sufficiently revealed by innuendo to occasion the writ for libel and a conspiracy charge, fought once again in the Old Bailey, the damages and legal defense fees of which so drained the *Brightonian* of revenue that it had to close down.

> He began his career at a huckster's stall,
> He eloped with the wife of a neighbour;
> At twenty he made an Old Bailey call
> And retired with six month's hard labour.
>
> Today he's too wealthy and too proud to thieve
> And moves on a high social level,
> And by aping great piety, makes us believe,
> He was ever bad friends with the ———.[13]

This subtle mixture of invective and suggestion is utterly characteristic of Blackburn; it is a tactic used to lure a victim into the open. Needless to say, the case which came up at the Queen's Bench Division in London on June 22, 1882, and lasted three days, drew enough dirty linen into the open for the Brighton town councillor in question never to recover his reputation.

Blackburn's Brighton days included other less hazardous enterprises, for he wrote the librettos for two operettas, *Disenchantment,* and *Angelo; or An Ideal Love*. Presumably these were in the buffo style of William Schwenck Gilbert of Gilbert and Sullivan fame, appropriate to the fashionable seaside spa with its Brighton Aquarium

The Weapon of Ridicule

Theatre on the famous entertainment pier. At all events, it was here that Blackburn came across the ventriloquist and magician Smith. As Blackburn's journalistic fortunes declined due to legal difficulties, so Blackburn and Smith devised a double act which Blackburn boomed widely in his paper, and which impressed audiences on the British south coast, avid for feats of sophisticated legerdemain and mind-reading, then much in vogue. Blackburn himself solicited the probe by the society gentlemen then investigating spiritualistic phenomena of the telepathic order. Only twenty-six years later, in 1908, was Blackburn to come clean about his intentions at the time:

> In the late seventies and early eighties a wave of so-called Occultism passed over England. Public interest became vastly absorbed in the varied alleged phenomena of Spiritualism, Mesmerism—not yet labelled as Hypnotism—and Thought-reading, now better recognised as Thought Transference or Telepathy. . . . I exposed several minor mediums, and on the whole was on very good terms with myself as a champion of common sense and an exposer of charlatans. . . .[14]

On his complicity in committing a fraud himself, by knowingly posing as the real thing, he remarked:

> My youthful vanity was flattered at the notion of my being able to hoodwink men of a vastly superior mental calibre to myself, and I venture to say that most very young men would have felt a thrill of exultation in the knowledge that they had been able to set at nought the wisdom of the wise. I don't say that there is anything commendable in this, but I do say the weakness is very human.
>
> To the gratification of vanity must be added another important consideration which I am certain has influenced many who have taken part in "spoofs" of spiritualists, the belief that one is helping to kill a ridiculous credulity by that most potent of weapons, ridicule.[15]

Whatever the rights or wrongs of this dubious sequence of dupings in Blackburn's early career—and voluminous evidence is available as to how he fooled some of the leading scientific and metaphysical researchers of the day, helping to drive one of them, Edmund Gurney, to an ignominious suicide—it emerges that Blackburn made no money from his maneuverings, nor did he significantly add to the circulation of the ailing *Brightonian*. His closeted telephathic demonstrations with Smith were held privately, without payment.

But what is worthy of comment about this episode is that it shows an interest in Blackburn which would become second only to his journalism and his career as a novelist—his dedication to the unusual subject of cryptology. His demonstrations of thought-reading with Smith were rigged by means of elaborate codes of stenographic-graphological signals. In later years in South Africa his esoteric knowledge of codes would stand him in good stead as a criminal investigator and expert witness on handwriting in many a court case.[16] Back in London in 1908 and in reduced circumstances it would also provide him with a new career as an inventor of a shorthand system.

The Blackburn–Smith conjuring fraud of 1883–84, however, is the only facet of Blackburn's career, and a minor one at that, to have received any attention, notably in an illuminating piece of biographical detection, a book called *The Strange Case of Edmund Gurney* by Trevor H. Hall.[17] This was adapted into a BBC-2 television drama by Ken Taylor, called *The Magicians: Edmund Gurney and the Brighton Mesmerist,* in which the role of Blackburn was played by the actor Richard Todd.[18] Yet, for our purposes, almost everything else about Blackburn is of greater interest. Hall and his assistants put little emphasis on the abundant examples of Blackburn's youthful intentions as a prankster, and almost totally ignore his subsequent career in South Africa which, after all, was to prove of unique interest, not to conjurers and illusionists, but to the literature of the colonial heyday.

Fleet Street and his Origins

When the *Brightonian* folded in 1884, Blackburn attempted another one-man satirical sheet, the *Brighton Figaro,* but this collapsed for lack of financial backing within a month; no copies are extant. Thereafter he enters an untraceable period. Some would say Blackburn was opening gold mines in China, some exploring the African interior from Senegal. Others speculate that he joined the Palestinian Exploration Society and made great inroads into the classical past, or circumnavigated the Mediterranean alone. But, given Blackburn's propensity for chaffing his idle listeners, plus the fact that there is no internal evidence for any of these adventures in his writings, we are forced to conclude, rather unsensationally, that he spent his missing years as one of the great anonymous journalists of London's

The Weapon of Ridicule

Fleet Street. Certainly, when he arrived in Johannesburg, Transvaal, in 1892, he had acquired a reputation as a smart Fleet Street man, a professional and proficient scribbler over newsprint. To his dying day his blood was full of printer's ink.

We might indulge in a little romancing here, Blackburn-style. In the shadow of St. Paul's Cathedral, outside the City of Westminster in a borough of its own, is the meeting place of the world's news networks, Fleet Street. On this corner, at Ludgate Circus, is a plaque to the memory of Edgar Wallace, another copy manufacturer who made his career in South Africa. Down a dingy alley is St. Bride's, the journalists' church, maintained on tithes paid by the press. On the Embankment is a bust of W. T. Stead, editor of the *Review of Reviews*, with whom Blackburn would have a spirited interchange about the former's championship of the imperial factor. The spirits of William Blake and Charles Dickens walk the foul corridors, grimed with fliers and scandal. Up Holborn there were music halls and variety palaces, and in the West End opera and melodrama. And so on and so forth.

Two details of Fleet Street journalism seem particularly appropriate to the Blackburn story. The first is that the golden inlay of the dome of the same St. Paul's bears a memorial in memory of the 4,300 sons of Britain beyond the seas—from Australia, Canada, Ceylon, New Zealand and South Africa itself—who lost their lives in the South African War of 1899–1902.[19] The second is that in the London *Daily Mail* archives—which are filthy dirty, being uncleaned since the bombings of World War II—their index of articles contributed with by-lines (which, unfortunately, does not stretch back to the nineteenth century) reveals at least one piece written by Blackburn (in 1915). This demonstrates that he had an open entry to papers as prestigious as the *Daily Mail*. The piece itself was about how to breed rabbits. Blackburn was at it again, never at a loss for a bright idea, never saying die.

All that can be said with any certainty about the Blackburn period post-Brighton is that Fleet Street was then the most important communications center in the world and that all the tides of empire washed through it. When Blackburn arrived in South Africa, eight years after Brighton, he was thoroughly aware of how to submit work to the mighty British press, although he was never a stringer or a full-time correspondent—and in this way he supplemented his income. He had also become a worldly man, who had acquired all the know-how to enter with assurance the wave of journalism that hit the Transvaal with its first newspapers in the 1890s.

Also, Blackburn certainly knew his London from the inside. Just as he was never a magistrate in the Transvaal (he was more of a magistrate's victim), so was he not a son of any fecund English clergyman in France. A search in St. Catherine's House, London, revealed that he was, in truth, a Londoner by birth.

Douglas Blackburn's origins were so poverty-stricken that he probably had reasons enough, once he had climbed up the British social classes, to conceal his humble beginnings. He was born south of Fleet Street, just across the River Thames. On August 6, 1857, it is recorded, Elizabeth Blackburn, formerly Ward, who sometimes gave her name as Ward Mount Edgcumbe, gave birth to a son named Douglas, whose father was called George Blackburn. He is described in the entry of birth as a journeyman leather-dresser.[20] The father, then, one above the apprentice stage in his profession, was a hireling who worked for daily wages in an abattoir.[21]

His son was born in their home, at 13 Lombard Street, Southwark. At that date, the names of the neighboring streets gave an indication of the shambles-type nature of this area of London: Morocco Street, Tanner Street, Lamb Walk. A few blocks south of Guy's Hospital and London Bridge, Southwark was no middle-class haven of learning and educational opportunities. There could have been no precedent in Blackburn's own family for becoming a writer. The abundant sympathy he shows in his novels for characters who, under the stringencies of poverty, malnutrition, illiteracy, and lack of privilege, try to "make it" into the professional classes would seem sufficient evidence for describing Blackburn's origins as similar. He may, in later life, have sounded as if he were the son of a clergyman and been educated in a classy private school, but there can be no doubt that he was neither.

The Transvaal Republic

Like many an underpaid British journalist in the world's metropolis, Blackburn went abroad to find his fortune. He chose to go south to the Transvaal, a land that advertised all the fervent activity of a gold rush and the prospects of an independent life-style in the forefront of newsmaking.

When, in 1892, he arrived in the land-locked Transvaal, then known as the Zuid-Afrikaansche Republiek, it was, in fact, to face a slump, an economic depression that aggravated social conditions that were far from golden and promising. The Transvaal itself was an ill-defined territory ruled from the city of Pretoria. It was presided over by the long-lived President Paul Kruger, whose granitic presence and style of autocratic government through a Volksraad, or House of Assembly, were renowned institutions through to the end of the nineteenth century. The Transvaal itself was a self-governing republic controlled by some 20,000 Burghers of the tenacious Boer stock which had migrated inland from the Cape at the southern tip of the continent in the 1830s and established their autonomy from British colonial rule. With the adjacent pocket of Boer territory, the Orange Free State, situated between the Cape and the Transvaal in central South Africa, the Boer regimes covered 170,000 square miles of land. Both republics, once on the outermost fringes of British colonial development, found themselves by the 1890s as enclaves in the way of the grandiose push of British empire expansionism to the north. By the time of Blackburn's arrival, the Transvaal was surrounded—around the north and west by Bechuanaland, which had become a British protectorate, and by the newly annexed Rhodesia, and by British Swaziland to the east. To the south, the Cape, and to the southeast, Natal, colonies well settled as British domains, were expanding inland.

British inroads into the continent were motivated by two waves of development—the discovery of diamonds near Kimberley in the Cape in the 1870s, and of gold in the Witwatersrand area in 1886. These events were not unconnected, for mining capital from diamonds flowed across the Transvaal borders to establish Johannesburg. This new mining camp was situated at the center of the gold reef, which runs west from Johannesburg to Krugersdrop in a band some eighty miles long. In 1886 Johannesburg, no more than a scruffy tent and shanty settlement, some thirty miles south of Pretoria, was declared a town, and by 1892 the first railway train had arrived on a branch line of that British line that was designed to run from the Cape to Cairo. The town itself, one of the fastest expanding centers of the colonial world—and one of the greatest gold-rush bonanzas of the globe—attracted to it from California, Australia, northern Europe, and England itself a population of prospectors, diggers, and mining engineers who, within years, were monopolised by financiers and managers from Kimberley. By 1892 the first crisis of gold mining was occurring—the awesome change of mining technique from surface washing and alluvial gold recovery, which could be undertaken by independent laborers with picks, shovels, and wheelbarrows, to the technique of recovery by heavy machinery demanded as the reef was discovered to slope sharply underground. Johannesburg is proud to boast, even today, of the deepest underground mining operations in the world; it was this necessity to sink shafts unprecedentedly far into the bowels of the earth which called for the inflow of speculators with capital and monopoly syndicates which ousted the independent digger. The issues that this trend brought to the fore—the recruitment of cheap black labor, the industrial revolution of gold, the anarchic and crime-ridden opportunism of such a social conformation—would become Blackburn's major subject matter as a writer.

But the tension was also building between Pretoria and Johannesburg, and in 1899 would explode into three years of warfare that would not only set the trend in modern military procedures, but would see the end of the stable era of Queen Victoria. The war would also utterly transform the nature and the structures of the Transvaal itself. This pre–Second Anglo-Boer War period, then, is Blackburn's own; no other writer has captured it in such detail and with such perception of the issues churning toward its destruction. Before the war there were no less than 110 goldmining companies operating on the Rand, employing some 11,000 black laborers, some 2,000 white foremen and compound managers, and all in control of the various mining enterprises—"the capitalist gangs," as Blackburn would frequently dub them. Chief shareholder in this operation was Cecil Rhodes, himself premier of the Cape Colony, who during the decade conducted expansionist operations north of the Transvaal by—to use the jargon of the time—pacifying Matabeleland and Mashonaland and creating his own personal kingdom, Rhodesia (now Zimbabwe). The Kruger–Rhodes conflict is the key to the period, for just as Kruger embodied the agrarian values of free-ranging Boerdom, so Rhodes epitomized the industrial expansionism that marched forward to take "civilisation" into the so-called backward parts of the earth.

One of the instruments of this civilization was the press. A daily afternoon newspaper like the *Eastern Star,* founded in Grahamstown in the Eastern Cape in 1871, literally rolled into Johannesburg on ox wagons in 1887 to become the *Star,* to this day one of South Africa's leading newspapers. When Blackburn entered the employ

The Weapon of Ridicule 15

of the *Star* on his arrival, it was to face two issues. The first was that he would not serve the mining interests that controlled the paper for long, and the second was that, like all his fellow Uitlanders, or foreigners, he had little prospect of being enfranchised as a Transvaal citizen. The right to vote in the Transvaal was reserved by the Volksraad for true "sons of the soil," the native Burghers, descendants of the Dutch who first settled the Cape in the seventeenth century. They had, however, occupied the Transvaal for only two generations. They were pastoralists, working in community units called commandoes, on horseback, to defend their small settlements across their vast terrain spread from the Vaal River in the south to the Limpopo in the north. The consolidation of the Transvaal Republic was still in its last phases in the 1890s, as the Boer policy of surrounding independent black tribal lands within the Transvaal frontiers and dispossessing them at gunpoint was not yet complete. Blackburn himself rode with the Boer commandoes from Pretoria on the campaign of genocide against Chief Magato in 1894. Classed as a temporary sojourner in British Johannesburg, Blackburn was perhaps to become more intimate with his rulers, the Boers, than any other journalist of his day; it is an entirely South African irony that the great chronicler of the last days of the Boer republic should be a working-class Englishman, one who sympathized with their egalitarianism (for whites and Boers only), and who despised, in common with them, the workings of the industrial revolution his own people were foisting on the pastoral arcadia that flourished so out of touch with the rest of the world.

Another so-called civilizing import was the music hall, that rolled into Johannesburg in prefabricated form along the other route, from the port of Durban in Natal. By the time Blackburn entered Transvaal journalism there was already a thriving entertainment industry in the spreading town. Here an eyewitness account of Blackburn's early days on the Rand, by a fellow journalist on the *Star,* Manfred Nathan, is useful:

A member of the editorial staff with whom I soon "palled up" was Douglas Blackburn, a man considerably older than I was—perhaps forty-five. He did the music and dramatic criticism. . . . With Blackburn I went to *The Shop Girl* at the Standard. . . . This company had a highly successful run. . . . Not so Miss Fortescue. She opened a drama season at the Amphitheatre in Harrison Street. Blackburn wrote a devastating notice of her opening performance, and her season came to a full-stop there and then—a remarkable instance of the power of the Press. Whether Blackburn had a secret grudge against Miss Fortescue I do not know. Born in Lowestoft, he had gone to Fleet Street, and I fancy had something of a chequered career there. . . . Often in the late afternoon he and I used to go to the bar of the Grand National, and his beady brown eyes would grow brighter and beadier, his nose would become shinier, and his moist mouth moister, as he told some anecdote of the past glories of Leicester Square . . . or of Mrs Langtry and the *debut* of Mrs Patrick Campbell. . . . [22]

Nathan himself was to become very much of a Blackburn protégé, and was the first and only historiographer of South African literature to give Blackburn his due in terms of space and critical assessment.[23]

To eke out his income, Blackburn, while still on the *Star,* became associated with a rival press group with a policy more to his liking. It was called The Press/De Pers, and run from Pretoria by Leo Weinthal, publishing in Dutch and Setswana. In English in Johannesburg it published in the form of a weekly tabloid review with a satirical tendency, called the *Moon.* As only two copies of the *Moon* are extant, one of July 1893 (vol. 1, no. 21) and the other of May 1895 (vol. 5, no. 117), and neither show an editorial masthead or give any indication of authorship, there can be no certainty as to how much of the *Moon* was of Blackburn's doing. Its policy, however, was typical of what was to come in the Blackburn story; the editorial statement of vol. 1, no. 1 of the *Brightonian* might stand in here as a likely summary: "Comment without egoism; criticism without acerbity or spleen; personality without offensiveness; and lightness without triviality,—and on these broad lines we intend to proceed, be the results either glorious success or honorable failure."[24] And, like the *Brightonian,* the *Moon* probably intended to enlarge beyond the conventionality of other local papers.

Although most of its achievement goes unrecorded, the *Moon* was the first of some dozen pre-war fly-by-night newspapers in the Transvaal, and gave rise to a tradition of satirical journalism which lasted, under a state of constant siege, well into the twentieth century. The *Moon* was also part of a larger British tradition of independent journalism which was to the press syndicates what the digger was to the monopolist. This tradition had been present in the Cape since the first major British settlement of 1820, when the first journalists and literary men, like Thomas Pringle, Andrew Geddes Bain, and William Layton Sammons ("Sam Sly"), arrived to tackle the continent, wit in one hand and prolific pen in the other.

But the man in the *Moon* himself, although critical of British policy, as all independent papers of the decade were, was markedly pro-Boer and was directly sponsord by the Kruger regime. This may be seen in the *Moon Annuals,* which Blackburn edited for De Pers in 1893 and 1894, the Christmas collections summarizing the year's events. These handsome volumes were sophisticated feats of printing, including engravings and color lithographs of Transvaal personalities and scenes. The 1893 volume has a flattering portrait of Kruger as "Our Grand Old Man at the Wheel" and lampoons Rhodes as the "Baron of Shangani and Bulawayo," stranded like Napoleon on an island labeled Matabeleland, with the caption, "Always on Her Majesty's Service." The same collection quotes an imaginary letter from Dr. Jameson, saying "in my humble opinion, Maxim bullets are a decidedly effective remedy for Matabele evils."

The annual of 1894 is also a pictorial spectacular, presenting the tranquil beauties of the wooded Transvaal, subtly underlining a sense of Boer achievement and harmony, and with little comment it endorses the campaign of the Boers against another so-called rebel chief, Malaboch, who was defeated in the Zoutpansberg. Predictably, he becomes a state prisoner in Pretoria, over whose head the Vierkleur (Four Color) flag of the republic waves in victory. This annual also contains a lengthy survey signed by Blackburn (his first acknowledged piece in South Africa). This is "The Beginnings and Development of Deep-level Mining at Witwatersrand," with detailed remarks about the success of the introduction of the cyanide process for extracting gold from the rock beneath Johannesburg. The impression the *Moon* sought to convey was that "progress" was not antagonistic to the welfare of the citizens and noncitizens of the Transvaal, and that all were welcome to seek bounty and an integrated, harmonious future. Blackburn was to turn sharply from this view in 1895.

In May of that year the syndicate that ran the *Moon* was liquidated and Blackburn reverted to full-time employment on the *Star*— Nathan's description of him dates from this time. One of the last editorials of the *Moon* talked of an Old and a New Transvaal, in the latter of which the Uitlander element of miners, traders, and commercial agents was rapidly becoming Africanderized under Kruger's benevolent sway. The *Star,* however, backed an imperial line, pushing for political rights for Uitlanders, who by then comprised a population of 35,000, far outnumbering the Burghers. Part of the *Star*'s campaign was to underline so-called grievances which the expatriate non-Boers were suffering under Pretoria. The only English-language paper in the Transvaal which opposed the *Star* throughout most of the decade was the *Standard and Diggers' News,* to which Blackburn would defect in due course.

Krugersdorp Days

The turning point for him was the crisis that struck on Christmas Day, 1895, and which by New Year's Day had realigned many of the tensions in the troubled republic. The Jameson Raid was made by a column of Bechuanaland and Rhodesian troopers, allegedly sent by Rhodes to alleviate British grievances on the Rand. They invaded the Transvaal during that fatal Christmas. This emergency is dealt with in detail in Blackburn's second published novel *(Kruger's Secret Service),* and will be discussed later. The effects of the Raid, which was stopped short near Krugersdorp by Boer commandoes at the Battle of Doornkop, were complex. For one thing, it threw off confidence in the Johannesburg stock exchange and introduced another slump in overtraded gold mining, which resulted in large unemployment on the Rand. Blackburn himself moved to Krugersdorp with an auctioneer friend and socialist, William Ramsay Macnab—who is often mentioned under his own name in Blackburn's novels—and they formed a "syndicate" (Blackburn's own mockingly grandiose description of their entrepreneurial resources) to purchase an ailing English-language weekly. The *Sentinel,* like the *Moon,* was attached to a pro-Pretoria Dutch paper, *De Voortrekker,* chief organ of the Independent Printing Company.

In Krugersdorp, frequently dubbed Devilsdorp by the pro-British press, Blackburn truly came into his own, or at least, since the *Sentinel* years (1896–98) are the most fully recorded of his career, he can be seen to come into his own in some detail. Macnab and Blackburn brought an improved printing press with them. Their paper's policy was "To tell the truth, the whole truth and nothing but the truth." But by November 1896, the *Sentinel* had already run into trouble. This came in the form of Kruger's New Press Law, designed to control the ferocities of the newspaper war which was eagerly being waged from one end of the Rand to the other. Basically, the law compelled articles to be signed by existing people, so that individual authors could be held culpable for their statements. Blackburn immediately reopened the *Sentinel* as the *Transvaal Sentinel*, with the identical editorial policy, "only more so." The 105-odd numbers of the *Sentinel* and the *Transvaal Sentinel*, edited by Blackburn and of his sole authorship, all but a few of which are preserved in the State Library in Pretoria, form the single largest source of Blackburn journalism, and are used extensively throughout this book.[25]

One of Blackburn's early editorials set the defiant, fighting tone of his admirable newspaper:

We insist that before a person shall be entitled to equal privileges with the original inhabitants of a country that he shall give some sign that he is prepared to make sacrifices if needed for the common cause. There is not a Burgher of the State who has not at some time shown by his actions that he is prepared to give this evidence of his right to citizenship. But what do the capitalistic gang do to prove their right to a voice in controlling the destinies of a country which they openly boast is only a temporary abiding place that will know them no more as soon as they have collected sufficient spoil to warrant their leaving. . . . This humbug is too transparent to deceive anybody, and it does not.[26]

At the time Krugersdorp was the third town of the Transvaal and, unlike Pretoria or Johannesburg, was a meeting ground of Briton and Boer. It was a market town where agricultural producers met mining employees in a relatively unpolarized mix. This was the type of environment in which Blackburn could flourish, unleashing his campaigns against humbugs, charlatans, opportunists, and plain crooks, taking polemics to court on the least pretext, and generally conducting his one-man battle for the rights of the decent common man.

The range of the small-town journalist had to be all-inclusive. He covered not only by-elections but fashion parades, transport problems, and murders and gossip, and the arts as well. The accumulated Blackburn village reporting reveals that his life was one long skirmish with one or another Sanitary Board, the predecessors of the modern Town Council. He was more than once given to inveighing against the "unsuitability of the night slop van,"[27] a cumbersome sanitary cart drawn by horses that emptied the outside latrines from a private lane running between the backs of houses in town, a lane which has a glamor all of its own in South African dorp, or village, life. He described his ramshackle residence in Krugersdorp as follows: "the mud-coloured house at the corner of Kruger and Human Streets and at the end of the atrocious bit of impassable foot path that runs past the office of the Road Inspector; stand no. 185, Krugersdorp, South African Republic" (*S*, September 30, 1896).

The saving grace of his campaigns was always his humor, his agile punning, and his ability to turn an epigram: "Jan hanged at Pretoria [on Saturday] for murdering Paul le Roux, died without a wriggle" (*S*, April 22, 1896). "Drought, locusts, rinderpests, Matabele and Reform Trial about fill the bill this week" (ibid.). "Rhodes's greatest deeds are generally performed when there is no one looking" (*S*, July 8, 1896)—this in the Ladies' Letter from Kitty to Kaatje. On the sinking of the ocean liner, the *Drummond Castle:* "About five hundred people were going home on the *Drummond,* but missed it" (*S*, July 29, 1896). Some of the quotables are even more colorful: "The three gentlemen who commandeered the piano organ on Monday and serenaded their friends and enemies at midnight are invited to repeat the business at certain houses, where a fine assortment of Law and Menzies' bricks are awaiting them" (*S*, August 19, 1896). The republican policemen, nicknamed Zarps (Zuid-Afrikaansche Republiek Politie), come in for a fair share of ridicule: "Another Zarp has suicided. Unfortunately it is generally the wrong man who does this" (*S*, October 7, 1896). Missionaries are another inevitable target: "A lunatic named Warrcott has left £40,000 to a Missionary Society" (ibid.). On October 19, 1896, when the *Sentinel* changes its publishing day from Wednesday to Monday, Blackburn devotes much of the issue to a lurid description of a portable brothel moving into town over the weekend. Nor was Blackburn partial to accepting unsolicited contributions: "We have no vacancies for 'ratty' poets on our staff" (*TS*, May 29, 1897). In December 1896, a Liquor Commission visited Krugersdorp and reduced the number of licensed bars and canteens from seventy-three to thirty-three.

Blackburn's life in Krugersdorp was perforce a public one. He attended the races, the patriotic Burgher rallies at the Paardekraal monument outside Krugersdorp, erected to celebrate the Boer victory over the British in the First Anglo-Boer War of 1881, during which the Transvaal freed itself from an attempt of the previous year to annex it from Natal and raise the Union Jack at Pretoria.

He attended the smallpox prevention committees, the wapenschouws—gymkhanas at which mounted Burghers showed off their arms—and the Masonic Balls. He was an adept pianist of the honky-tonk sort, and acted as master of ceremonies at many a cultural evening, particularly at the International Society, and his charitable duties included arranging a free visit for the children of the dorp to a circus entertainment, given by the *Sentinel* syndicate, when "seven hundred and fifty youngsters testified to the fecundity of Krugersdorp" (*TS*, September 9, 1896).

He was offered bribes by liquor racketeers beating the prohibition on supplying low-quality booze to black mine laborers, by diamond and gold smugglers, by treasure hunters and pickpockets, all of which he genteelly declined in favor of exposing the bribers in the columns of his newspaper. A recurring theme of his Krugersdorp days is his chivalry in defense of the good name of ladies. Assaulting those blackguards who defamed a lady's reputation landed him more than once in court,[28] and on one occasion this led to a dawn duel with pistols. The duel was called off at the last minute by the challenged, but only once seconds had been called and the course paced out.[29]

The English journalists of the day remembered Blackburn's career on the *Sentinel* as having been uncompromising in its exposure of the petty corruption, nepotism, and palm-greasing of the Burgher administrators. Blackburn's understanding of the Taal, or Afrikaans as the language would become known as, was more than efficient. "Doughty Douglas" (*TS,* May 15, 1879), as the *Boksburg Herald* dubbed him, had several run-ins with Boer officialdom. We may guess that Blackburn used the forum of debate of the newspaper and the court room for more than honorable rectifications of petty insults and innuendoes. His habit was to manipulate public discussion on issues of public interest through these channels into the open, and thereby, often at great personal cost and through spending many a night in jail—he referred to the Krugersdorp jail as his "kennel"—influencing people and winning supporters and friends.

But while Blackburn was frequently quoted by the English press as an exposer of Boer corruption, the other facets of his independent-minded social criticism were largely ignored. He had in common with the British newspapers in the Transvaal a contempt for Kruger's attempt to muzzle the press in October 1896, when even the *Star* was closed down, only to reappear as the *Comet* the next day.[30] But where he differed from the imperial press was in his critique of the workings of British capitalism on the Witwatersrand. Here Blackburn was very much of a lone crusader. In his "Open Letter to Mr W. T. Stead," for example, he remarked:

> I would give something to see your face if brought in personal contact with a representative crowd of Rand "Imperialists" and "empire builders." Believe me they are not the noble characters you appear to imagine them. And worst of all you are, unconsciously I believe and hope, championing the cause of the curse of civilization, the ascendancy of the capitalist interest . . . the enslavement of the workers, the crushing out of the poor man and the perpetration of countless deeds of cruel injustice. . . . (TS, April 1, 1896)

So much for Rhodes and the colonial secretary, Joseph Chamberlain. And so far as the Jameson Raid was concerned, Blackburn called it a "Rob Roy expedition" of "unscrupulous professional plunderers" (TS, December 31, 1896).

Blackburn conducted a campaign through the *Sentinel* to discredit the financial houses of Johannesburg and their mining interests across the subcontinent. A fellow spirit of his, the Cape liberal, Olive Schreiner, was also volubly active in this cause. Her polemical novella, *Trooper Peter Halket of Mashonaland,* was often approvingly quoted by Blackburn in the *Sentinel*. The cause of Schreiner's and Blackburn's anti-imperial vehemence was their sense of the war clouds being on the horizon. Blackburn resorted to every means in his power to promote harmony between the two controlling white populations of South Africa. First, he assaulted the military ethic, the gunboat diplomacy which, during Queen Victoria's reign, was so reliably successful that Britain colonized no less than one fifth of the world. For Blackburn, Rhodes was merely a new member of a whole gallery of wholesale butchers, and he saw that "such trifles as honor, breach of faith, oppression, and brutal monopoly, are not considered worth setting out against the fact that Rhodes has now added more territory to the British Empire" (TS, February 13, 1897).

Second, Blackburn circularized every influential editor of an English-language newspaper, journal, or magazine in the world with a pamphlet called "If There Should be War," which, as it turns out, was a fairly accurate forecast of the war to come. He alerted the press to the accumulation of armories across the Transvaal and

The Weapon of Ridicule 23

to Kruger's self-defensive measures taken in case of further British encroachments, remarking that no British army was capable of dealing with Boer artillery, rifle marksmanship, and camouflage tactics in a terrain they knew only too well. Such factors indeed led to many British military disasters in the closing months of 1899. Further, Blackburn unashamedly asserted the rights of Boerdom to its territory, and praised Boer society as classless and tribally cohesive. Like the Irish, Blackburn maintained, no Boer could be subdued or colonized permanently. He believed in the alternative of working out an integrated racial partnership.

Another part of Blackburn's campaign enlisted sympathetic Uitlanders by printing for them reports of conditions on the Rand which could be cut out of the *Sentinel,* pasted on post cards, and sent to all corners of the globe. One such ingenious announcement reads as follows:

The Transvaal Sentinel published an appeal to the English, American and Australian press to warn miners and artisans against emigrating to the Rand. It points out that the stories of high wages and general prosperity of the working population have been grossly exaggerated, and are circulated by the capitalist for the purpose of overcrowding the labour market and bringing down wages to bare existence point. . . . Competent workers in every branch of industry are walking the streets and even sleeping out by the hundred. . . . Johannesburg is the dearest place in the world to live in. A glass of beer costs 6d., spirits 1s., 2 lb. loaf of bread 9d., eggs 3d. each. . . . On the top of all this comes the fact that the mining companies are making a united effort to reduce wages all round. Under these circumstances the man who emigrates to the Transvaal deserves all he is likely to suffer. (*TS,* May 8, 1897)

When there was a lock-out of miners on several of Sir J. B. Robinson's mines around Krugersdorp during this crisis time, Blackburn actively entered politics, addressing miners' protest meetings. He advocated calm, the avoidance of violence, and organization into Trade Unions for unified representation to the mines' managerial committees. The *Sentinel* published in slip form procedures on how to plan "closer union" (a term which, a decade later, was to refer not to trade unionism, but to the unification of South Africa). A trade union, the *Sentinel* wrote, "may not have been needed before, but it will sorely be needed very soon. The history of trades-unionism all the world over has been one of triumphant success. The Rand miner's union, to embrace every branch of mine worker, should be the success of the century" (*TS*, May 8, 1897). The trade union movement on the mines was not, in point of fact, to gain any strength in the Transvaal until after the war, and Blackburn's attempts to oppose capitalism with a frontal attack from the socialist quarter were not then destined to have any tangible success.

Blackburn himself was not a doctrinaire socialist, although he had read with care all the socialist "rags," as he referred to them, of his day. When, later in his career, he was tackled by a Labourite pro-Trade Union candidate for support (in West Kent in 1918) he replied that he would vote Labour for housing reform, for sanitation, education, recreation, care of infant and mother, but not for trade unionism itself, which he saw as yet another self-enriching process, this time in the interests of the suppliers of labor. He resolutely affirmed that "the true and useful function of a journalist is to act as a public interpreter . . . the journalist must be regarded as an impersonal medium only, with no views of his own."[31]

As the leading member of the Transvaal "reptile press," Blackburn's own policy was to assert not the socialist principles of organization and resistance with which he was in full sympathy, but the best of British individuality. In short, he resisted all forms of oppression, be they from the Tory warmongers or the Boer oligarchy. Ben Viljoen, his successor on the *Transvaal Sentinel,* in his valedictory editorial, described Blackburn's policy as follows:

The Sentinel . . . has consistently opposed hypocrites, has fearlessly exposed shams and frauds and has never been deterred by fear of consequences from criticising those in high places.

The mighty millionaire along with the ordinary Zarp came in for impartial attention and while the editorial chair was occupied by that experienced journalist, Mr Douglas Blackburn, some excellent work was done in the direction of counter-attacking the effects of exaggeration and misrepresentation too often indulged in by the Jingo organs. . . . The sentiments of *The Sentinel* could never have been mistaken; they were redolent of republicanism and the paper could not be accused by its most bitter antagonists of adopting time-serving tactics commonly called "sitting on the fence" out West and in closing down we would take the opportunity of emphatically reiterating our confidence in Republicanism as the one safe form of Government for South Africa. (*TS,* August 24, 1898)

Owing to its inability to "balance income with expenditure" (ibid.), the *Transvaal Sentinel* closed down with that issue, and an impoverished Blackburn moved back to Johannesburg for the last days of an era collapsing into battle.

Johannesburg and the Fin de Siècle

The year 1899, celebrated elsewhere in the world as the extravagant fin de siècle—the apex of the Age of Decadence and of Aestheticism in the arts, of poets like A. C. Swinburne and dramatists like Oscar Wilde, and the triumphant climax of the age of scientific inventiveness and its practical applications in terms of global transport, communications, and machinery—was, in Johannesburg, a year of austerity, of insecurity, and finally of mass panic. The destabilization of the economy through lack of confidence on the part of the British investor, the flooded labor market, and the oversubscription of dozens of small and unviable mines, was leading to crisis conditions of unemployment and the resultant gangsterism. The steady polarization of the two dominant white races proceeded, with Jingoes on the one hand, Burghers of the state on the other. It was also a year when intrigue was at its peak and, as Blackburn was to point out, the Transvaal's secret service—nonexistent a mere decade before—had quadrupled its number of employees since the Jameson Raid.[32]

In 1899 the *Standard and Diggers' News* employed Blackburn with a "roving commission,"[33] and what he contributed to this working man's daily was unsigned. His free-lance connection with the *Standard and Diggers' News* was probably a financial play-safe, for on his return to Johannesburg Blackburn immediately launched another satirical independent weekly, and almost immediately ran into trouble with it. A report in the *Krugersdorp Standard* bluntly records the following under the heading *"Life* in Court": "Mr Douglas Blackburn charged Johannesburg Police Court on Tuesday December 20th, 1898, with contravening the Press Law by neglecting to register his newspaper *Life*. . . . (Laughter.)"[34] He went to prison for an unspecified period, rather than pay the £2 fine.

Only one issue of *Life: A Sub-tropical Journal* has survived.[35] It is no. 12 of March 4, 1899, and contains this scathing advice to a rival editor: "Give it up, Joe. Running libellous sheets requires more than the capacity to kick. It needs a bigger capacity for taking kicks." In this issue of *Life,* Blackburn maintains some of his equanimity as a social commentator, regarding the scene with his usual Olympian impartiality. But the old weapon of ridicule seems now to be more of a hacksaw than the elegant rapier of his earlier broadsides. It would seem that Blackburn's own detachment, his relaxed poking fun at all and sundry, had somewhat radicalized. Presumably, on his return to Johannesburg he felt that the situation called for stronger comment than before. A sense of anger has stolen into his humor.

For the Kruger regime he had this to offer: "The next session of the Raad is to be conducted with more regard to the religious professions of the State. In short, the motto 'Let us prey' will be kept more prominently in the foreground."[36] And on their passing of a new Ontucht (Immorality) Law, designed to curb the activities of the local Sodom—that is, Johannesburg, with its three hundred houses of ill fame and 1,200 public prostitutes—Blackburn had this to remark: "Sunday in Johannesburg was a day of much swearing and law-breaking, and to-morrow will see hundreds of orgies in private rooms." His offensive was against naivety and the hypocritical presumption that passing an ever-increasing number of prohibitive laws would remedy the conditions that called them forth in the first place.

But for the British faction he reserved an unprecedented amount of venom. In *Life* in an open letter to the new editor of the *Star* he launched this jeremiad:

Sir,—I have not the pleasure of your acquaintance, though I know you very well by repute, which reputation, I am glad for the sake of South African journalism, is an enviable one. For that reason, and actuated by that spirit of freemasonry which is one of the redeeming and most pleasant features of the profession you have adopted, I purpose giving you a little advice. . . . You will at first stand aghast at revelations of cold-blooded outrages on all that Englishmen of your calibre are taught to regard as sacred. Betrayal of public trust, the undisguised acceptance of bribes and the general exploitation of the public for private benefit will at first appal and disgust you, and the probability is that your better nature will revolt and express itself in words that burn; but you won't write a second leader on the same lines. Public opinion will be dead against you. You will be laughed at as a Quixote and chaffed over your inexperience, and taken home to dine sumptuously by a man who laid the foundation of his wealth by buying stolen diamonds. . . . I believe you have paid some attention to American politics. In that case, revive your recollection of the methods of Tammany Hall in New York, and the Trusts of Chicago, and apply the lesson to Johannesburg. You are coming to help and justify the grossest, most material, unscrupulous and sordid community that civilization has produced. You will be required to voice the unholy sentiments and aspirations of a class whose motto is "Eat, drink and acquire, for to-morrow we catch the next boat."

From the rhetoric of this tirade one may extract a succinct portrait of Blackburn himself. He is the Quixote conducting his impossible campaign in a world in which evil has run rampant. It is a bold and fruitless role to play, but one that is not without a glorious kind of honor of its own. In the South African newspaper wars of the time, there is no other figure who is such a moral ideologue, and such an uncompromising loner.

The South African War

With the outbreak of the Second Anglo-Boer War, the time for tirades and philippics was over. The war itself came quite predictably, to the day. In June 1899, President Kruger met the High Commissioner of Cape Colony, Sir Alfred Milner, in Bloemfontein, where they conferred on issues of common interest in an effort to avert hostilities. The conference broke apart on the matter of votes for the Uitlanders in the Transvaal. Kruger held out for a seven-year residence qualification; had this been accepted Blackburn would have been eligible for naturalization and enfranchisement as a citizen of the Z.A.R. Then, as Blackburn puts it, "Event crowded on event, corruption, scandals, Government defiance of High Court judgments, ill-treatment of Cape boys, a reign of terror in Johannesburg, owing to the inability of the police to cope with the criminal element. . . ."[37]

On October 9, 1899, Kruger addressed an ultimatum to the British government, demanding the withdrawal of British troops building up on the Natal border. The demand not being complied with, the two nations were formally at war two days later. Blackburn had underestimated the number of Boer rifles ready to take the field at 30,000, for when the combined Free State and Transvaal commandoes invaded across the Natal border there were 80,000 rifles in the service of the combined republican cause.

Here we lose a direct link with Blackburn's precise movements. An invidious choice faced him: neutrality was clearly an impossibility for a British citizen in a country at war with his own. He could, as a Boer sympathizer, have enlisted with the commandoes to fight his own private civil war with Britain, as many Uitlanders did in commandoes from Australia, Scandinavia, Ireland, Russia, and Germany, the latter with the Kaiser's tacit backing. But Blackburn was a noncombatant to the end, and assumed the role of war correspondent behind the enemy lines. It is unclear, however, what the nature of his relationship with the Kruger administration was at this time. Certainly, for many years he had interpreted encoded telegrams and deciphered espionage communications for their secret service in Pretoria. Also, in his Krugersdorp days, he had always favorably reviewed the Krugersdorp Volunteers, those Boer mounted forces who were particularly proud of their military band, which, incidentally, had been practicing British bugling calls for some years so that, in the event of war, they could confuse the enemy.

Lacking any evidence to the contrary, we have to rely on Blackburn's word, and we know how unreliable that is. In a letter to his publishers, Blackwood's of Edinburgh, he was to claim: "I have been on commando with [the Boers] in two Kafir wars and had the specially good fortune to be the only English correspondent on the Boer side up to [the Battle of] Elandslaagte, where I was at the request of certain Hollanders put under arrest and conveyed over the border to Delagoa Bay [in the neighboring Portuguese territory of Mozambique]."[38] Elandslaagte took place on October 22, and was the first of the disastrous setbacks which checked the British troops, inadequately prepared in their advance. We may assume that Blackburn had at least a fortnight's experience of the war from the "other side" at close quarters—this much is perfectly clear from *A Burgher Quixote* as well—and will have to leave the question of his allegiances and sympathies open.

After Delagoa Bay Blackburn reentered South Africa at Durban on the British side, and from 1900 until when he left the country in 1906 he was based almost entirely in Natal. For the *Times of Natal* in Pietermaritzburg, the capital of the colony, in October, 1900, he compiled an immensely thorough war number, designed as a souvenir of the first phase of the war. This detailed the sieges of Mafeking and Kimberley in the Cape, and of Ladysmith in Natal, and the disastrous first months of the war which resulted in British defeats at battles like Magersfontein on the western front. Daily reversals lead to Christmas, 1899, being dubbed the blackest celebration in the history of the British Empire.

With the dawning of the new century and the late arrival of British troops from the commonwealth, the tide of the war slowly turned. Bloemfontein, the capital of the Orange Free State, was occupied, and Lord Roberts marched on Johannesburg and—the ultimate objective—Pretoria, which, by June 1900, was under British subjection. Blackburn's very full account of this first phase ends with the battle for supremacy in South Africa won by the combined British forces, and with Kruger and his ministers in flight down that same railway escape route to Delagoa Bay. It was not foreseeable when Blackburn put his compilation to bed for the *Times of Natal* that a second phase of the war—that of guerrilla resistance and sabotage on the part of the Boers—would drag on for another two vicious years, nor that with the arrival of General Kitchener the "mopping-up" operations would introduce to modern warfare the most notorious of strategies, the use of concentration camps and the use of noncombatant civilians as military targets. The final statistics were to be appalling, rivaling any other of Queen Victoria's "little wars": 27,000 Boer women and children dead, 21,000 imperial forces and sympathizers dead, and 14,000 blacks dead—those noncombatants who fought on both sides—in this, the last of the gentlemen's wars.

At all events, from New Year, 1900, Blackburn had firsthand experience of the war on the Natal front. From the impeccably unemotional account he gives of the Natal campaigns around the besieged Ladysmith—relieved only in February 1900, after 120 days—it is quite hard to believe that Blackburn saw any action. In his compilation of the war number, his sources are war correspondents of the Central News Bureau, Reuter's, the *Daily Mail* (London), the *Daily Telegraph,* and the *Times,* as well as several South African newspapers. Yet there is no feeling of his own eyewitness authentication of any battlefront exposure. To an unprecedented extent, the South African War offered a field ground for the news correspondent in touch with Fleet Street. We need mention only the names of some of the noted reporters who tackled the story day by day—Winston Churchill, Edgar Wallace, Rudyard Kipling, and A. Conan Doyle. Apart from the bulk of on-the-spot reporting, the war was also to produce a generation of "war poets"[39] and "war novelists."[40] From Blackburn's own work in fiction it is abundantly clear, however, that he did also have firing-line experience of British action.

In later life Blackburn was frequently given to advertising the fact that he was grievously wounded during the war at the skirmish of Pieter's Hill in one of the bungled attempts of the British forces to break through to Ladysmith, in January 1900. Six years later, when he returned to London for a few months of medical treatment, he wrote to Blackwood's: "I have the satisfaction . . . of having contributed a useful & encouraging item to surgical knowledge, namely—that a bullet through the bladder & left kidney is not necessarily fatal. It has however seriously affected my riding capacity and a South African who cannot ride is much in the position of a dumb orator" (*EiA*, 44). Whether the bullet that struck our Colonial South African—as he had now taken to calling himself—was deliberately fired at him as an armed aggressor and enemy, or not, will probably remain unknown.

Here we might feel Blackburn's self-proclaimed war heroics need to be a bit deflated. As his collaborator, W. Waithman Caddell, wrote to an associate of the *Tonbridge Free Press* after Blackburn's death: "his joining our forces and *fighting* at [the Battle of] Colenso!—This we (S. Africans) have chaffed his head off about. I think, for News purposes, he did get attached to an ambulance outfit in Natal but nothing more heroic."[41] Nevertheless, by late 1900 Blackburn had retired from active participation in the war, in whatever capacity, and was an invalid in recuperation. And, as a novelist, he was able now to turn his experience of both sides of the battle zone into uniquely insightful fiction.

At Loteni Valley and in Natal Colony

The place where he was offered a semiofficial job in the Natal Criminal Investigation Department was a remote and most beautiful one, the Loteni Valley center of a Native "location"—that is, a black tribal reserve area—under the overpowering range of mountains that dominates the heart of South Africa, the Drakensberg. Loteni Valley snuggles between spectacular limestone and granite outcrops at the foot of one of the highest, often snow-clad peaks in Southern Africa. The Loteni police post was no more than a collection

The Weapon of Ridicule

of two mud huts. Its nearest center was Pietermaritzburg, and communication by ox wagon between this remotest outpost of empire and the capital took two weeks, there and back. Scattered white farmers and traders in the area were wont to make the trip only once a year with their harvests. It was the perfect job for a man in whom bad health bred reclusive tendencies.

The Loteni post was, nevertheless, at a crucial crossroads, for in the mountains above was the British protectorate of the Kingdom of Basutoland (now Lesotho), with its alpine, stock-raising culture. To the west was the Nomansland of the Griquas and Pondos, only colonized by Natal as late as the 1890s. In the foothills below the post lived a large Zulu population scattered there after the Zulu Wars of 1880–81 and only partially absorbed into white Natal. Here Blackburn began a new life. He was probably, like any lone white official in the boondocks, a bit of everything—policeman and detective, adviser to local black chiefs and the white resident magistrate, justice of the peace, and commercial dealer. Possibly also, at the age of forty-four, he had decided for the first time in his life to give up active journalism for a while and to live by his pen as a novelist. Perhaps he was merely associated with, and not dependent on, the settlers and administrators whom he was to describe in such critical detail.

To the rest of South Africa, however, by June 1902, and the end of the war, the alarming news was that Douglas Blackburn was, literally, dead. He was widely mourned as yet another casualty of the carnage. This is his riposte:

One of the drawbacks of residing in a district 40 miles from the nearest railway, five days between posts, and only hinted at on the official maps, is that one does not know what is going on in the world. It was not until I read in the [*Natal*] *Witness* of the 12th. inst. the announcement of my own death that I knew that event had happened; but as [we] have only just heard of the declaration of peace and the transposition of the City Fire Brigade Chief, our behind-the-age ignorance of current events may be fathomed.

As an old pressman I am naturally cautious about contradicting statements made in print, so I will content myself with asking your readers to receive with caution your statement as to my decease, and suspend judgment until I can produce more conclusive evidence than my bare word that you have been misinformed.[42]

After praising the restorative, health-giving virtues of Loteni Valley, "this Never-Never Country," he concludes in the same piece: "The air is pregnant with inspiration, and I am laying it under contribution and endeavouring to crystallise it in the pages of my long-promised sequel to *Prinsloo of Prinsloosdorp*, which will see the light as soon as the public require a relaxation from the absorbing but exhausting records of the Coronation."

Amid these serene surroundings, Blackburn was in good humor and poised at the beginning of the high-living Edwardian Age, ready to launch his first novelistic triumph, *A Burgher Quixote*. The covering letter that Blackburn sent to Blackwood's with the manuscript included these comments: "I have founded a style in South African literature, which it is my earnest desire to maintain and improve. . . . At the same time I feel justified in admitting that I regard this book as the work of my life and shall be prepared to stand or fall by it" (*EiA*, 35).

The first decade of the 1900s proved for him to be more than a record of the odd publishing success. When *A Burgher Quixote* came out in June 1903, it ran into one colonial and two British impressions, evidently bringing him satisfactory financial rewards. In 1904 it was followed by the successful *Richard Hartley, Prospector*. In 1908 he published *I Came and Saw* and *Leaven*, and the same year saw a popular reprint in paperback of *Prinsloo of Prinsloosdorp*. Soon Blackburn began to receive considerable critical attention from the British and South African press, though now it was in terms of appreciation of his work as a novelist who specialized in South African subjects. Gone was the old scallywag contentiousness of all his attitudes struck in the days of the now-defunct South African Republic. Yet his heart, and his raw material as a writer, remained based in that lost, corrupt paradise which, of all the postwar writers, he chronicled and recorded in the minutest, most loving detail.

In the only known Blackburn correspondence, that between him and his publishers of the time, Wm. Blackwood and Sons, a contented, middle-aged Blackburn now comes to the fore, a painstaking literary man as absorbed in his style as in his subject matter. He revisited Krugersdorp once, in December 1904, where he recovered his old typewriter, and seems to have had some role to play in the reconstruction programs underway during the British occupation of the Transvaal. When in 1908 the Transvaal once again elected its own representative government, it was soon, as a leading member, to enter the coalition of the four provinces into the Union of South Africa, achieved in 1910.

In Natal, during those years after the peace and pre-Union, Blackburn returned occasionally to daily journalism, particularly as a parliamentary reporter in Pietermaritzburg. An old friend of his from Krugersdorp days, William Hills, recalls:

> Few of the members of the Press Gallery of those days, who included another future novelist in the person of Perceval Gibbon, will ever forget the happy time we spent. In fact, so bright was the conversation that on one occasion the sergeant-at-arms came up to request the Press Gallery to modify the conversation in the reporters' room, which opened off the gallery, as it seriously interrupted the work of the House. . . .[43]

In 1904 Perceval Gibbon, probably at the suggestion of Blackburn, also published a novel with Blackwood's, *Souls in Bondage,* the first South African work on the theme of miscegenation, or interethnic sexual relationships. Set in steamy colonial Pietermaritzburg, *Souls in Bondage* features two semireputable British journalists given to drinking sprees and fraternizing in the "native quarters." It is difficult not to conclude that the older one of them is an oblique portrait of our seedy Douglas Blackburn. Blackburn was to match Gibbon with a miscegenation novel only several years later in *Love Muti,* which in turn features a younger man in the coils of a lurid interracial love tangle.

One of Blackburn's watering holes in Pietermaritzburg was the plush Botanical Hotel, at which he inscribed a copy of the Colonial Edition of his *A Burgher Quixote,* in the possession of the present writer, "in recollection of early days and later nights (Aug. 10, 1904)." But, apart from this detail, evidence of Blackburn's life in Natal Colony is frustratingly sparse. Once again we enter a period of great anonymous reporting. There were independent satirical weeklies sprouting in Natal at the time, but it would seem that Blackburn had no hand in them. One of these of which we have a reasonably complete record, the *Prince,* founded in Durban in 1904, shows no trace of Blackburn.[44] It was highly conservative in its criticism, mostly given to fomenting phony "black peril" scares, and moved up to Johannesburg in 1905. Despite the fact that Natal, unlike the Transvaal, had always fallen under British copyright laws, and thus copies of entire runs of Natal publications are on file in the British Library, Blackburn—now at the height of his literary fame—seems least in view as a man.

There is a connection between Blackburn's earnings and the pattern of his publishing in this period. With *Richard Hartley, Prospector* out from Blackwood's, the relationship between him and his publisher seems to cool and even become curt, for reasons that are obscure. The last letter in the Blackwood's archives in Edinburgh from Blackburn is dated July 15, 1908, and it seems to tell the truth:

> You will probably have noticed that Alston Rivers Ltd. is publishing a novel by me.
>
> I should not like you to think me ungrateful or discourteous after all the important assistance you have given my work.
>
> The M.S. of *Leaven* was with the copyright of my *Prinsloo of Prinsloosdorp* sold in 1897 to a Mr Dunbar who published (through MacLeay) *Prinsloo*. His representatives have since transferred both to Rivers & I have no financial interest in either.
>
> I am busy on a new and novel work which I hope to submit for your consideration shortly. (*EiA,* 45)

Blackburn seems to have become caught in an unpleasant double-bind situation. If he had sold the manuscripts of *Prinsloo* and *Leaven* outright in 1897—at a time when the *Transvaal Sentinel* was in economic difficulties—he would have gained no further financial rewards from their publication (in the case of *Prinsloo,* republication). Yet it is not certain that *Leaven* was completed by 1897; although its subject matter is prewar, its style seems to date from much later, probably from Loteni Valley days. Then, the very attractiveness of *Leaven* as a publishing proposition was caused by the success of *A Burgher Quixote* and *Richard Hartley* with Blackwood's, publisher of Joseph Conrad and many other well-established writers. The new novel he then offered the reputable and prestigious Blackwood's must have been *I Came and Saw,* which evidently was rejected, presumably on the grounds that Alston Rivers, Ltd., was in direct competition with them with *Leaven* and *Prinsloo.* In the end, *I Came and Saw*—the fruits of Blackburn's brief return to London in 1906— came out from Rivers as well, and it seems that Blackburn had well and truly wrecked his career. Neither Blackwood's nor Rivers kept Blackburn in print, and the latter was to go under in due course. Thanks to this deadlock situation, Blackburn's fiction was to disappear off the bookshop shelves almost as soon as it had made its mark.

Blackburn finally left Natal and was back in London in 1908, his *annus mirabilis* that saw three novels and an abundance of articles out. Whereas for all his working life in South Africa he had been an Uitlander in the Transvaal, and in Natal a Home-born man, he was now to experience the strange reversal of no longer being a true Englishman. By 1908 he was fifty-one, and his brief creative period—that produced six out of seven novels—was mostly behind him. When in 1915 he published a seventh and last novel, with another publisher of little longevity, Everett's, he had not adapted his skills to writing about the prewar world of London. *Love Muti* calls on experience of Natal in 1906, and it would seem that there his creative impulse ran dry. It is true to say that Blackburn's entire output as a creative writer derived from South Africa between the years 1895 and 1906, and that, in one sense, he was a uniquely South African writer. Yet, as he approached retirement, he obviously chose to turn his back on South Africa and return home.

Edwardian London and Tonbridge

Apart from the literary glory—attached to no solid financial results—that Blackburn gained on his return to England, his last twenty years seems to have been shabby and, to say the least, somewhat poor. Edwardian London seems to have enjoyed its vogues, not least of which was the popularity of A. Conan Doyle's detective stories. In a now demolished area of London, Blackburn set up shop with a younger South African, Captain W. Waithman Caddell, advertising all sorts of schemes that show how colorfully Blackburn could live off his wits.

In 1909 Blackburn and Caddell published a handbook, *The Detection of Forgery*, for the use of bankers, solicitors, magistrate's clerks, and all handling suspect documents. This 77-page work is a most thorough enquiry into the finer nuances of holography, doubtless of absorbing interest to those expert in graphological fakery at Scotland Yard. It was the only such handbook in print at the time and was meticulously researched by Blackburn, as of old, in the British Museum Reading Room. From 13 Charlwood Place, London, S. W., Blackburn and Caddell lived by giving opinions as to the genuineness of documents and by tracing the authors of anonymous letters. One of their sidelines was an interesting trade in literary and historical autographs, although there appears to be no record of any such treasures they may have handled.

In 1911 Blackburn and Caddell furthered their partnership in detective work by producing the true oddity, a joint-autobiography. The work was called *Secret Service in South Africa* and published by Cassell's. "Autobiography" is not an entirely accurate description of the book. Although every event described in the work is attested to by one or the other contributor, this enormous tome (380 pages) reveals virtually nothing of the private lives of the two men whose story it is. Their purpose in writing it, however, was clear enough:

> This volume has at least one feature not possessed by the majority of cognate works. It has not been written to attack or defend any party or policy.
> The authors have been prompted by two main reasons. First, they have had peculiar, and in some respects unique, opportunities for close association with the persons and events dealt with. Secondly, the opening of a new chapter in the history of South Africa with the establishment of the Union seems to warrant a valedictory review of some of the less-known events and conditions of the Old Regime before they become indistinct and hazy, and possibly perverted in the re-telling.[45]

The term "secret service" may be very widely construed in this instance to cover the inside story of every branch of Transvaal life in which Blackburn and his partner were involved.

Again we have a mystery here. Captain Caddell is described as the chief repatriation magistrate for the West Rand during the British Occupation, and yet there is precious little in the work itself to suggest Caddell's hand or experience. For those interested in Blackburn, however, the work is a trove of good information, for it collects together and collates almost all the material he wrote as a factual journalist. It is also out of this range of anecdote, news story, eyewitness account, background piece, and feature article that Blackburn's fiction was made. It is almost safe to say, in trying to assess the authorship of much anonymous material about the Transvaal, that if it is not in *Secret Service in South Africa*, it is not by Blackburn. For him, the compilation of this weighty testament was, as it turns out, a final stock-taking of the rich middle years of his creative life in South Africa.

The Weapon of Ridicule

And, in a sense, it was the end of him. After 1911 and *Secret Service in South Africa* Blackburn did not have much that was new or newsworthy to offer the world at large.

By 1912 the Edwardian Age of lavish life-styles and daring morality seems to have wound down into one last fling, as pre–World War I shortages became evident. As paper rationing was imminent in London even then, Blackburn and Caddell—formed into Blackdell and Co.—took ingenious advantage of the crisis by announcing a system of shorthand that would save both paper and words. Their scheme was not destined to "catch on," and the secretaries and reporters of the time chose to adopt the method of Sir Isaac Pitman. Probably this proved an unequaled disaster for Blackburn, as the printing of *Print Shorthand: The Office System,* with its practice pads and diagrammatic examples, must have called for a large outlay in capital. Apparently, though, the Blackdell system proved popular with stenographers in Dublin.

Stories of Blackburn sleeping out on park benches as a London tramp date from this time.[46] It must have been in circumstances like these that he posed as a representative of the South African Farmers' Association and put forward hare-brained schemes to advocate homegrown rabbits as a source of protein to combat war food rationing in 1915.[47]

In the same year, and somewhat opportunistically, he slapped together with cut and paste an account of the life and death of Nurse Edith Cavell, whose end was the cause celebre of the day. Here is Blackburn's own comment written on the flyleaf of his *The Martyr Nurse: The Death and Achievement of Edith Cavell,* his last published book:

This booklet was manufactured in almost record time. It was suggested by the publisher [Ridd Masson Co.] at noon on Sat Octr 30 and the last proofs were passed on Tuesday Evg Nov 2. It was arranged that a foreword shd be written by W. S. M. Knight, but he had not time so my first chapter was commandeered & signed by Knight as *his* foreword. Thus are books made.[48]

Books "manufactured" to catch a ready market—in this case the memorial service in Cavell's memory, which was a mass demonstration of outraged British patriotic feeling—might be made that way, but one does not feel that the sensationalism displayed within its flimsy 6d. covers reveals the true Blackburn. For once, it seems, he lost his calm control over a contentious situation, and broke into a furore of anti-German invective. It was Nurse Cavell, the subject whom he was honoring, who at the moment of her execution by a German firing squad as a British spy, said, "Patriotism is not enough. I must have no hatred or bitterness towards anyone."[49] We may contemplate Cavell's statue off Trafalgar Square, or her stuffed dog in the Imperial War Museum, thinking that Douglas Blackburn should have been the last man to make capital out of the horror that put her humanitarian values to death. Then the war entered its phase of conscription and Kitchener called for a million men.

Here we reach Easter, 1916, that fatal date in the history of human warfare, at which time the maverick subject of this biography at least found his final home—in Tonbridge, Kent, on the *Tonbridge Free Press*. There he spent the last thirteen years of his life in stability and contentment. We are back to where we began, with Blackburn the raconteur and bar-room entertainer, the man whose weapon of ridicule had only temporarily deserted him during the blackest days of World War I. According to Croft-Cooke, his room in Ashburnham Road had survey maps of the Transvaal pinned to the walls, and he described to the young poet how constructing a novel was as hard as building and launching a battleship; no final, unpublished manuscript has come to light, however.

By the time Blackburn was buried in Tonbridge in 1929, the memories of his achievements in South Africa and of his irreplaceable novels that flowed out of it, had become a trifle aggrandized and shot through with a resigned mixture of inspiration and leg-pull. One of the most moving tributes to him, however, came from a "Fellow Worker" in the small party who attended his interment:

He was not only interested in the routine of the composing and machine rooms, but was ever ready to understand and appreciate the difficulties of others, with many a kindly word of pleasure when things ran smoothly, while mishap or delays were never magnified or unduly noticed. He was very generous in his utterances, and it can be said that a word of thanks from him was worth a great deal. The same remark applies to his "copy"— he was an ideal writer, generous with the papers he used, and exceptionally straight-forward. The compositors could always understand, and know that by "following copy" he was sure to obtain the desired result, a "clean" proof. In private life Mr Blackburn was the same, and the floral token which described him as "a man" briefly and correctly stated what we all think. (*TFP,* April 5, 1929)

He was a reliable pressman to the end; his last column on the *Tonbridge Free Press,* concerned as ever with civic efficiency and the rights of the common citizen, appeared two days after his pauper's funeral.

Chapter Two
The Adventure Antihero

This chapter considers two early works by Douglas Blackburn which interdepend on one another and which raise common issues. They are *Kruger's Secret Service* and *Richard Hartley, Prospector*. Both are novels, though in the case of the former considerable energy is spent in demonstrating that this is not so. Both were written early in Blackburn's Loteni period of retreat from 1900 to 1902. Although they are not his first works of fiction, it is convenient to group them together here, as will become apparent.

Kruger's Secret Service—the very title promises intrigue—was first published in 1900 by John Macqueen in London. It was part of the spate of works which flowed from the newsmaking South African War, commenced in October 1899, and very much in the headlines of the British press during the early months of the new century. We can imagine that Blackburn had little difficulty getting the work published, as it falls into the category of eyewitness information and, in a sense, "cashes in" on the topical events of the day. As there are no longer any publishing records of a company named Macqueen, we can have no greater clarity on the circumstances under which *Kruger's Secret Service* came into print.

Published a year after Blackburn's first novel, *Prinsloo of Prinsloosdorp*, which similarly appeared to catch the same wave of public interest in affairs in the Transvaal, *Kruger's Secret Service* was likewise published pseudonymously. To this day its author appears in catalogs of Africana books as "One Who was in It." Blackburn assumed this attribution probably to strengthen the idea that the book was an expose, or a behind-the-scenes record, and this promised sensational but true revelations. Choosing anonymity, Blackburn could also remain free to tell the truth as he saw it with impunity. The result of this, however, has meant that in some libraries the work has remained classified as an historical account, and is seldom, if ever, read for what it truly is—a scrupulously contrived work of fiction, and one of the more bizarre works to have emerged out of the war.

The same is true, but in a very different way, of *Richard Hartley, Prospector*. Following the success of the publication of his third novel, *A Burgher Quixote* (1903; the sequel of *Prinsloo* [1899]), Blackburn seems to have come out of cover: *Richard Hartley* was published under his own name, and on the title page he is billed as the author of *A Burgher Quixote* and of *Prinsloo*. We may assume that those works were by then reasonably well-known. By the time of *Richard Hartley*'s publication, the name of Blackburn presumably meant more to publishers than the news value of the subject matter of the works themselves, and from here on he will no longer assume disguises. Anyway, by 1904–5 and *Richard Hartley*'s first appearance, the war—already two or three years over—had lost its value in terms of up-to-the-minute news, and there is little attempt in *Richard Hartley* to give to the world any sensationally new angle on the events. The Jameson Raid and the war itself, which are burning issues in *Kruger's Secret Service*, fade into the background in *Richard Hartley, Prospector*—although they are pivotal in the story, they are treated more as historical events than as contemporary reportage.

The two works which we have here give us two versions of very much the same action—one written by the anonymous Blackburn the journalist in the heat of the moment, and the other at some remove in terms of time and place, and with a sense of greater detachment and perspective. We might go as far as saying that what was urgently rushed in *Kruger's Secret Service* and impossible to conclude was subsequently redone by Blackburn the novelist in an altogether more temperate and relaxed phase. Also, these two works chart the development of his artistry, and we are here privileged to see how his thinking on the uses and functions of fiction was generated. Between the years of 1900 in which *Kruger's Secret Service* was completed (the last dated action in the novel is the relief of Ladysmith) and the 1904 of the completion of *Richard Hartley, Prospector*, Blackburn put a large amount of thought into the possibilities of fiction in South Africa, and evolved a unique and singularly appropriate solution to the problem of shaping the dramatic events of his time.

Kruger's Secret Service

This is an oddly hybrid work. Presented to the public as a work of fact by a pseudonymous writer who claims an "inside" knowledge of his subject, it could only have gained strength and meaning when read as an "authentic document." Judging by the success of the anonymity ploy in the case of *Prinsloo of Prinsloosdorp*, which also posed as a work of documentary fact, we can assume that Blackburn had some experience of the effects that could be achieved on a readership by erasing the neat boundary line that exists between the way we read a work of "fact" and the way we read a work of "fiction."

Kruger's Secret Service is a careful imitation of a work of fact—to the extent of including an illustration of a telegram (facing p. 54), purporting to be addressed to the (blanked out) author of the work. In style it is densely packed with the kind of details that give it a sense of authenticity. Only once we are some way into it, do we find the small give-aways that mark it as a work of quite a different order, but then only if we are reasonably familiar with Blackburn's idea of a joke. If any reader is taken in by the strategy that Blackburn here employs, we need only point to that illustrative telegram— the handwriting on the form of the Telegraafdienst of the Z.A. Republiek is Blackburn's own; it could not have been sent from Cape Town to any real and now untraceable secret service agent who, as the work pretends, has decided to come clean. When Blackburn is playing his games, it is remarkable how the methods of detection which he himself pioneered in the Transvaal secret service can serve the ends of a literary detective as well.

To the relatively small reading public of the Transvaal familiar with Blackburn as a writer and public personality at the end of the 1890s, it must have been pretty obvious who the author of *Kruger's Secret Service* must have been. But 1900 in the Transvaal was no year for leisurely perusal of any revelations of the security secrets of a regime then in disorder and in flight. Blackburn's publishing of the work in London means that he had other intentions—he meant to reach the reading public back Home with this release from behind the lines. This way he devised an effective means of saying what he felt was timely and apposite about the causes of the war. So unorthodox is the type of thinking that went into *Kruger's Secret Service* that there is even a case to be made for its being an antinovel, a work which in many profound ways sabotages the norms and expectations of the novel itself.

Kruger's Secret Service, then, is a novella (or an antinovella, if we apply the common definition) with a hero who is intent on making his uneasy confession anonymously. The confession stretches for no more than 35,000 words, covering the days of the Jameson Raid over Christmas, 1895, through to early 1900, and so deals with the chaotic period leading up to the war and its first disasters. The narrative itself jumps from event to event without apparent continuity, and is arranged into chapters more by subject matter than by accumulative plotting. In the very middle, for example, the sixth chapter out of nine branches off at a tangent to the main action to establish the relationship between President Kruger's secret service operations and the illicit liquor business flourishing during this period in Johannesburg. Only by reading with extreme care may we discover any thematic connection between this and the rest of the material. The apparent randomness of the narrative line is part of the effect of the work as a whole.

The key to the novella is this main character, who has every reason not to give his name. We know that he is English-speaking, but it would be false to assume that merely because of his language he is automatically in sympathy with the British cause. He poses as a not very skilled artist:

> it is somewhat difficult for a man of no literary training like myself to express [emotions] in such a simple and straightforward fashion as shall prove their truth and authenticity to all. At the same time, the number of thoughts, ideas, and obscure sensations that throng through a man's mind . . . are so extraordinary and so complex, that a transcript of them, thoroughly written out by an artist in language, who had actually taken part in a campaign, would prove one of the most vivid and enthralling books ever written in the world.[1]

Here the narrator is apologizing for his inability to convey with any fidelity the crowded complex of feelings which assail a man on a battlefield. But this example holds good for the novella as a whole. He pretends ineptness and inexperienced naiveté in literary procedures throughout. For Blackburn, meanwhile, this type of inexperienced narrator is the ideal storyteller. The plain "unvarnished" quality of his tale is more effective than any "literary" account with all its fine shadings, analysis, and sense of the dramatic. The reader's willing cooperation in believing in the fiction as fact is subtly played on in this way.

Needless to say, the work as a whole is not at all lacking in artistry. It has always been a common satirist's ploy to use any means to render the reader credulous, and to appeal to him or her with a supposedly genuine line. Blackburn's sense of irony, here pitched at a very low but well-sustained level, balances credulity against a sense of criticism. While we believe his narrator phrase for phrase at one level, we also actually see what he does not see at another. As a result, any details our hero gives away about himself must be taken up with a degree of critical skepticism. Whenever he is most assertive of his British patriotism, we are to look for the ironic truth beneath: circumstances will generally reveal his motives are not patriotic at all, but merely opportunistic. Whenever he makes a claim about his noble motives, we can be sure that Blackburn means us to see a certain ignobility beneath, and so on. Once that technique of ironic distancing is established—and this method of writing is Blackburn's stock-in-trade—the work itself can proceed, richly and amusingly, to reveal a quite different set of motivations from those which the narrator intends to show us. The true exposure of the novella is not at all of what the narrator thinks—of Kruger's secret service in the last days of the republic—but of the moral state of life on the Rand in the last few years of the century, and its inevitable results.

Blackburn's narrator's first sentence outlines the major event of the book to come. He was recruited into the Transvaal Secret Service to effect the most unimaginably awful crime, the assassination of Cecil Rhodes, the same Rhodes whom Mark Twain, in Pretoria shortly after the Jameson invasion, described as follows: "In the opinion of many people Mr Rhodes is South Africa; others think he is only a large part of it. These latter consider that South Africa consists of Table Mountain, the diamond mines, the Johannesburg goldfields, and Cecil Rhodes."[2] A work which announces such a bold plot as the killing of a living British historical character, the figurehead of empire, sets up certain immediate expectations. We imagine a work of intrigue and suspense to follow, and also imagine that the confrontation between the killer (or author) and the Colossus (Rhodes's moniker) will be the climactic moment of the book. None of this is the case, however. Our faulty narrator continues: "In those days I was engaged in business in Johannesburg, in partnership with a friend. One morning, while strolling down to our place of business, we discovered to our astonishment that the streets were full of armed men" (*KSS,* 6).

This bemused, disconnected style is maintained throughout, always falling into an air of innocent astonishment, always promoting the idea that everything in the course of the action happens by accident. The narrator is always the victim of the whims of fortune and forced to improvise. In short, he is the perfect picaresque figure.

But Blackburn has him swear more than once that he represents more innocents than just himself, innocents who are the victims of "a lawless state of society" (*KSS*, 8). Referring to the events that occurred in the streets of Johannesburg as the news was broken of the impending Jameson Raid, he says: "I do not say that this is an accurate sketch of the facts as they actually were. But I do say that this is an accurate sketch of the feelings of ninety-five per cent. of the working population of Johannesburg" (*KSS*, 9). *Kruger's Secret Service,* in a unique way, is the view of the "working population" of English-speakers of the events which were buffeting about their heads and affecting every facet of the life about them.

Significantly, as is the case with our hero, the system drives them well beyond the fringes of legal behavior into situations of greater and greater criminality. Like Cervantes before him, in his (anonymous) picaresque novellas about the foundation of urban centers in Spain, Blackburn has a precise moral sense of the nature of economic pressures on the individual in a threatened position. It is not hard to predict that the view Blackburn promotes in the novella is one of the working class man being squeezed out of a living by the "capitalist gang." In *Kruger's Secret Service* it soon becomes apparent that it is not the Pretoria oligarchy that is public enemy number one, but the warmongers and schemers of the narrator's own side, Rhodes himself being chief among them.

The narrator of *Kruger's Secret Service* is all set to bring to the attention of the reader the "unofficial" version of the factors that caused the war, and to show their effect day by day on the hapless and powerless working man. Our hero of necessity embarks on a course of action which, by any definition of the word, is strictly unheroic, and his adventures form the core of the work. If they are "adventures" at all, they constitute a number of retreats from the challenges of fortune—this is not the stuff we associate with heroes in general. Nor is the central theme of *Kruger's Secret Service*—the matter of allegiance.

Our hero joins Major Karri Davis's Dismounted Australian Corps, a ragged bunch of the unemployed who are impressed to defend Johannesburg from a supposed Boer threat. (The real threat, of course, is the Raiders.) He has this to say about his motives:

I was an Englishman, and a loyal British subject, and perfectly ready to do anything in my power to advance the cause of my country. I, too, was a business man, depending on my business from day to day, and I suddenly found my business ruined by the political convulsions introduced by the Reform Committee. I had to do something to earn my support. Of course, it was the first reason that weighed with me much more seriously than the second. (*KSS*, 12–13)

But of course, to us, it is the second that we see weighing much more than the first. The Johannesburg Reform Committee's trumped-up insurrection of "loyal British subjects" is pulled off by the offer of generous payment to the out-of-work. At one pound sterling a day, our hero earns all of nine pounds from the entire Jameson Raid scare, and for nine pounds the Johannesburg Randlords and plutocrats extract from him the following: he trains a platoon in military drill, patrols the streets to maintain a curfew, cleans up the dens of vice known as skittle-alleys and shebeens, expels Russian Jews in the illicit gold business in a most tactfully handled and underplayed pogrom, smuggles arms from repositories all round the city to a central arsenal, and enforces a stringent lock-out of black laborers who supposedly constitute a threat to law and order. All that for nine pounds, plus—Blackburn adds with neat irony—a bottle of champagne and a cigar each evening.[3]

After the Raid scare is over, and Dr. Jameson and his corps are behind bars in Pretoria, our hapless hero tries to return to his line of business, only to find a second accident divorces him from his resources. On February 19, 1896, there was a catastrophic explosion in Johannesburg, which occurred when in the midday heat two goods trains, carrying between 56 and 60 tons of dynamite for use in blasting on the mines, collided. In historical fact this accident killed 80 people, left 700 injured, and made some 1,500 homeless. Like all disasters in Blackburn's world, the effects are felt most by the underdog, in this case the mixed railway suburbs of Fordsburg, Vrededorp, and Veldskoendorp, interracial ghettoes situated near the shunting yards. It spread further devastation across Johannesburg's shantytowns and brickyards, changing the face of the city, and naturally added to the jumpiness of two population groups living in close proximity on a footing of prewar tension.

The grim comedy of the Rand precipitates our witness into a succession of ever-increasing disasters, as one would expect from the picaresque formula. As he remarks, "I was becoming ripe now, as you can easily imagine, for any desperate adventure" (*KSS*, 107), and it is the sight of his only enterprise—his small share in a "winkel" or trading store—blown to smithereens, without any hope of compensation, which drives him into the central action of the work. This is his step by step enlistment into the Burgher secret service which at first concentrated its efforts on spying out any further armament buildups in the Johannesburg area. So corrupt is this secret service, protests our spokesman, that espionage and counterspying proliferate within it. Every secret agent uses his wits to outdo the next man for a bigger reward.

From here Blackburn's ironies compound with great effect. Before the assassination attempt, our hero is put through many trials, the first of which is burgling the very house of the man who first recruited him into the secret service, by which he proves his "fidelity" to the Kruger regime.[4] He sells out his best friend, an inventor manufacturing a new type of machine gun, even though he claims he is in love with the man's daughter. He travels across one border after another, posing as a representative of a consortium of business interests, liberally supplied with ready cash, spying out the extent of the British military buildup against the Boers. Of the secret service itself he nevertheless has the most ignoble opinion:

I wish to emphasize this repeatedly, that the corruption of the Transvaal is such that practically every man in the service was a traitor. No man could trust his neighbour, and, consequently, the Government was put to tremendous expense in order to see that its underlings did not present false reports, but conduct their business in an honest and efficient manner. (*KSS*, 107)

Yet the Secret Service Bureau, in its state of disorganized panic and unreadiness, was "perfectly ready to shell out money to our heart's desire" (*KSS*, 109). With facts and figures, however, Blackburn shows us that Kruger's financial resources were miniscule compared with the inflow of British capital to the Transvaal; in point of fact, the Volksraad was ruling a country that was bankrupt.

It is in conditions such as these—the upheavals of the sudden South African industrial revolution, causing a chaotic breakdown of the age-old social system of the Boers—that our hero acts out of dire necessity with all the resourcefulness of his kind. All easygoing norms of morality and loyalty are completely inverted; to survive he has to become a traitor and—for such is the nature of picaresque fiction—we applaud and even admire him each time he goes for the main, and only, chance available to him.

Thus we eventually come to the assassination atempt on Rhodes. Here, rather than recording the underside of social history, it seems that Blackburn is quite transparently inventing fiction. This incident in the plot was doubtless inspired by a true event which occasioned Blackburn's considerable polemical wrath. The figure to be the target was not Rhodes, but President Kruger himself. The advocate of assassination was no less than that most eminent adventure hero of the day, H. M. Stanley, the same American journalist Stanley who rescued the missionary David Livingstone from the heart of darkest Africa with the immortal phrase, "Dr. Livingstone, I presume." Blackburn reported the incident in the *Transvaal Sentinel:* "That exploding windbag, H. M. Stanley has advocated the assassination of President Kruger. . . . At the Rand Club, [Stanley said,] 'I *quietly* suggested a corrective of this incongruous and unprecedented condition of things, and said it lay in the saying, "It was expedient that one man should die for many" ' " (*TS,* February 9, 1896). Blackburn's own comment on this quiet suggestion was that it was "as foul and disgraceful an incitement to treason and assassination against the ruler of a friendly power as ever emanated from the Anarchist press," and he saved a last broadside for the Rand Club, nest of the Reform Committee, for not calling Stanley to immediate account.

In *Kruger's Secret Service* the suggestion of Stanley is reversed. Only the chicken-liveredness of our hero, assigned by Dr. Leyds, head of the Transvaal Secret Service, to do the job, averts the death of Rhodes. This great reversal of the book occurs simply because our man once he is in Cape Town imagines that, instead of poisoning the Colossus, he might well stand to gain even more by turning allegiances again, and warning Rhodes of the attempt:

I spent a very restless night thinking over the matter. It was not only that my instinct warned me that I should not compromise myself . . . but I had also other reasons for not giving myself away to any human being without some adequate return. My intention was when I brought the matter before the notice of Mr Cecil Rhodes, to procure not money from him indeed, but some adequate patronage as a reward for my services. (KSS, 124–125)

Our hero, it turns out, is not rewarded at all, for "Mr Rhodes at that time was on the point of sailing to England" (KSS, 126), to be acquitted from charges of complicity with the raid he had instigated. Our adventurer who has double-crossed the Boers, and thus laid himself open to grievous trouble on Rhodes's behalf, continues: "I do not know how far his memory will extend back, considering the multifarious interests and concerns to which he had at that time to devote his attention, but I think it is not unlikely that he will remember that I wrote him . . . a letter amplifying to some extent the information which I had given him" (KSS, 126). The letter in question is used by Rhodes to summon up a fervor of anti-Boer sentiment in Britain, and our man has had his greatest reversal yet.

Here Blackburn's satire becomes awkwardly obscure. It is possible that, while Rhodes was alive and all-powerful, Blackburn dared not conduct his fictional satire as openly as he might have desired. (The same is true of *Prinsloo of Prinsloosdorp*, which is remarkably guarded when it comes to satirizing Kruger himself.) Despite the protection of anonymity, Blackburn was still subject to actions of defamation of character. To sidestep this and to continue the accumulating development of his novel, he resorts to the somewhat oblique tactic of going underground in his style into buried symbolism. The relevant section (chapter 7) is the most tantalizing passage in all of Blackburn. It works without any clear line of implication, by contrast and juxtaposition alone. Without pointing any of the parallels, Blackburn expends no more than a curt few hundred words on the climactic encounter between our narrator and Rhodes. He then cuts directly into an elaborate and lengthy description of a visit to Robben Island, at that time a leprosarium and lunatic asylum in a quarantine area in Cape Town's Table Bay.[5] This visit is presented for no apparent reason, in a breezy style of reportage, as if it were a chunk of local color brought in as an intermission. Perhaps the narrator himself (or at least we are meant to believe this) sees no connections between the horrors of lunacy, the crawling disfigurements of leprosy, and the state of South Africa at the time. Madness and disease, however, are apt metaphors for the social scene Blackburn wishes to describe.

The central symbol in this sequence is described as follows:

> I remember several old women, for example, gaunt old creatures, with frowzy hair hanging down over their faces, shrieking and walking up and down, gibbering like a lot of monkeys, in a yard or coop similar to a chicken run, only larger. One lady in particular I noticed, walking up and down a line which she had drawn on the ground; first to one end of it and then to the other, never deviating by a hair's-breadth from this route which she had mapped for herself. And they told me in the asylum that she would do that the whole time she was allowed out, till she was called in again. The moment she went for exercise in the morning she drew this line. What the idea in her poor old disordered wits may have been nobody could tell, but she seemed to think is was a duty incumbent upon her to draw that line in the dust every day, and march up and down like a sentry, not erect, however, but with bent shoulders, staring at the ground and mumbling to herself. (*KSS*, 153)

The obsessive line drawing of the times, to use Blackburn's metaphor, the fixation on marching, on duty, on failure to see the significance of mad actions—all this, symbolically interpreted, leads to our hero's next reversal in this maddest of mad worlds. He is now not offered any quiet retirement in England or wherever turncoat spies should be sent, but enlisted into a British plot to assassinate half the leading members of the Transvaal secret service. With grim irony, the entire assumption upon which the book is based—that British are righteous and Boers scoundrels—is finally reversed. Our hero is now a victim of a double-bluff as vicious as any he himself has tried to pull.

This satirical point made, Blackburn lets the plot fizzle out at this moment, and his book collapses, just as the historical situation collapsed into the war. The last chapter of *Kruger's Secret Service* has our anonymous little man in action in a volunteer corps on the British side, and it is in this "fratricidal war" (*KSS*, 201) that he makes the disheartened comments about his ability to express the finer shadings of emotion felt by a man in battle, quoted above. Once more, however, history has cast him as the luckless schlemiel, the unfortunate buffoon whose best endeavors prove fruitless and whose personal integrity is compromised by a situation bigger than himself. Blackburn's method is pretty blunt; the narrator almost immediately ends up in the front line, firing at his friends on the other side. Here the irony is not as carefully extended as Blackburn was able to do in later works, and much of the impact of the early campaigns of the war is dissipated in featureless documentary detail. His descriptions of daily military life, nevertheless, are among the finest accounts in the literature, equaled only by Edgar Wallace's *Unofficial Dispatches*.

The work recaptures some of its earlier force, however, in the following poignant and cruel incident. One night, when our narrator volunteers to go out with an ambulance party to the Boer lines to collect the dead and wounded, he observes:

> It was curious as we drew near the Transvaalers to hear voices addressing us in perfectly good English:
> "Hullo, old chaps, coming out to hunt for your men, eh? Let's give you a hand."
> Naturally enough we had not too much time to waste with our kindly hosts for the time being, but it was really curious to see men who had been trying to shoot each other, drinking out of each other's bottles and even partaking of coffee from the same pot. I can vouch and testify that this is what happened to me that night. I was offered tobacco by the same bearded Boers who were sitting in a circle round a camp fire of theirs. Some very warm and very comforting coffee was prepared, and I was given a good swill of it, just as if I had been one of their own men.
> They volunteered to come out and help us, as I say, in hunting for our wounded, and one of them seemed particularly anxious to attach himself to me. I thought he was up to something, but did not venture to talk freely or to question him until we had got off by ourselves. . . . And then he revealed to me the secret of all his trouble. It seemed that he was a man of English descent, who had settled in the Transvaal, and who (or whose father) had become a naturalised burgher and a subject of Paul Kruger, and as such of course, he had been commandeered to serve with the Boer forces in the field against men of his own flesh and blood. (*KSS*, 198–99)

With this kind of insight into the war as it affected men Blackburn closes his work. For his narrator the end involves catching some disease which invalids him off the fields of carnage into the arms of the Natal hospital services, where for four and a half months (that is, until Easter, 1900) he rises and sinks in delirium and nightmare, trying to resolve the conflicting allegiances and loyalties which fight within him. His conclusion is that he can only praise the healing hands of medical orderlies. Finally, he returns to England, for which he has this strange caution: "I may mention, by-the-by, that a good many of the servants of the Transvaal Government . . . are scattered throughout the British Empire . . . and only the day before I wrote these words I met one of them face to face in Holborn" (*KSS*, 170). These words seem openly threatening; Blackburn seems to be saying that traitors are bred in one's very midst. Covertly, *Kruger's Secret Service* would also seem to be very close to Blackburn's own autobiography.

With the publication of *Kruger's Secret Service* Blackburn meant to show that the matter of choices across national boundaries was not a cut-and-dried one, and that within the heart of many a man the drawing of lines had forced a necessary duplicity, a dual allegiance that attempted to embrace both sides of a battleline. His resort to satire in desperate circumstances was in the interests of depolarizing that battleline, of finding reason and truth in a world gone insane with rodomontade and sloganeering, of demystifying the myths of power which he saw as causing boundless individual human suffering.

Richard Hartley, Prospector

Blackburn's second adventure novel, *Richard Hartley, Prospector,* uses substantially the same background as *Kruger's Secret Service,* but it is worked out on a far larger scale. The reason for this might well be that it is told by an objective, third-person narrator who has access to a far wider scope of events. Perhaps in *Richard Hartley, Prospector* Blackburn temporarily abandons the first-person account because he feels it to have a narrow, partial perspective; at any rate, this novel rather panoramically sweeps across a far greater range of characters and events.

The main burden of the tale is carried by two characters. The first is a British youth by the name of Graham Wilmot. The novel opens with him contemplating the work's main setting, the Witwatersrand, from the beacon at Paardekraal, erected by the Boers to celebrate their successful overthrow of the British annexation of the Transvaal in the 1870s. The date, now, is a few weeks after the Jameson Raid, and that fact alone promises the reader an analysis of the tension-ridden period that was a panic-stricken intermission before the outbreak of the Second Anglo-Boer War in 1899. Wilmot is poised at this historical moment, at the center of a battle-scarred landscape.

The action of the story that follows would not itself tell us much about the nature of the novel, but, in summary, it goes as follows. In pursuit of a wounded owl that flaps to earth in an old mining adit, or shaft, Wilmot discovers a concealed Maxim gun, obviously hidden as a result of the raid and the Boers' efforts to disarm the British supporters of the Rand. With the Maxim are several thousand rounds of ammunition. Wilmot's first impulse is to earn a reward for giving away the location of this hidden arsenal, but he then encounters the other leading character of the work, Richard Hartley himself.

Hartley is no greenhorn newly out in Africa, no tenderfoot, like Wilmot; in fact, his long-standing prospecting business has fallen on hard times and he is a desperate man. As the bonds of mateship are forged between these two characters, Hartley evolves a plan to smuggle the massive gun through the British lines in Johannesburg, through the Boer security network around Pretoria, and up north to one of the last "native" pocket kingdoms, that of Chief Magato who reputedly needs to buy armaments to defend himself from invasion by Boers. Magato himself has a legendary calabash of diamonds to pay out, these having been smuggled off the Kimberley diamond fields by his own migrant labor tribesmen. All but the last sixty pages of this 363-page novel concern the elaborate subterfuges to which Wilmot and Hartley resort in order to make delivery of the Maxim and claim payment.

Complications are legion. First, the gun itself is without one crucial part, the firing block. In order to manufacture a replacement part, Hartley and Wilmot call in the aid of a mine foreman and inventor, Adam McQueen (a character adumbrated in *Kruger's Secret Service*). (William Ramsay Macnab, the Krugersdorp socialist, is also brought in in his own person to help.) The technical complications postpone the export of the gun for the best part of a year, during which we follow both Hartley and Wilmot on their several adventures around the Rand, the former in search of capital to finance the transport of the expedition, the latter in search of a mining engineer whose expertise will assist McQueen in the reassembly problems. Concealed in a workshop on a West Rand mine, the gun costs more to maintain than their combined resources can meet, and they recruit money in various ingenious ways.

The second problem posed by the gun is its massiveness. In solving their transportation problems, Hartley and Wilmot fraternize with a rural Boer family, far from the wicked cities, from whom they plan to hire a sturdy ox wagon. Here a complication arises as Hartley, a middle-aged man not given to any but the strictest regime of continence, disturbed by occasional outbreaks of liquoring, falls seriously in love with the Boer patriarch's daughter, Clarie, despite the attentions paid her by a somewhat uncouth Boer widower and neighbor, Johannes Smeer. To resolve this romantic deadlock, Hartley hires Smeer for the expedition; all he is to know is that they plan to search out new mineral sites in the far north. Smeer, Hartley, and Wilmot form the inextricably linked trio which sets off with the gun, disguised as a newfangled piece of drilling equipment, on Smeer's wagon drawn by a team of sixteen. The route north is beset with various difficulties, not least of which is evading outlying Boer commando members, suspicious of any Uitlander expeditions into the heart of the dark inland. The heavy gun constantly threatens to burst out of its casing; the concealed ammunition alone weighs two tons. At one treacherous crossing of a drift, the nature of the wagon's cargo is revealed, and a complicated battle of allegiances ensues between the British axis (Hartley and Wilmot), the Boer controlling interest (Smeer), and the unpredictable factor of the "native" transport riders employed by the expedition. The appeal of money, however, outweighs any sense of the enormity of their treasonable mission as gunrunners.

With their arrival at the Magatese headquarters in the Zoutpansberg, Northern Transvaal, the gun is sold for a handful of diamonds far in excess of its value, and the return trip is started. Almost immediately, despite their scrupulous division of the spoils, the trio begin to fall out, despite the fact that they are mutually threatened by a party of secret service agents who occasionally give signs of themselves. One night Smeer is brutally murdered (by the agents), and Wilmot's suspicion falls on Hartley. This disintegrates their relationship, and Wilmot is struck with fever. In an attempt to find medicine to cure Wilmot, Hartley temporarily leaves the wagon, and Wilmot defects. They never meet again. With his and Wilmot's share of the booty, Hartley returns to Clarie. Suspected there of the murder of Smeer, Clarie rejects him and, with warclouds gathering, to avoid being hunted down by the Smeer family, by Clarie's father, and by the Boers in general, Hartley retires to an inaccessible part of the Drakensberg in British territory.

Most of the action of the war itself is bypassed and, in the concluding pages of the novel, a desperate Hartley, having found no new mineral deposits, emerges from his retreat to locate Clarie, now a prisoner in a British concentration camp. He secures her release, their love is tempered by their mutually ruinous experiences, and they invest his substantial gains from the gun expedition in a farm in the long-pacified savannah of Natal on the Transvaal border. The last pages of the novel act as an advertisement to Wilmot to return and claim his share in their new settlement. The able McQueen is the one who joins them, and the work ends with Mr. and Mrs. Hartley and their manager set for a life of mellow peace and prosperity as horsebreeders.

That is an outline of the plot of *Richard Hartley, Prospector*. The story hardly sounds different from adventure romances in general written about the opening up of inland and the establishment of a settled population on the frontier of many a British territory of the day. In part, the point of *Richard Hartley, Prospector* is the very typicality of the events in it. The novelty of this work does not lie in its use of plot and action, for Blackburn seems to be using the predictable quality of the plot as the basis of a work which is other than predictable in effect. *Richard Hartley, Prospector* is more a parody of the adventure romance genre than a mere copy of it, and it acquires its strength and interest from being so. By November 1904, when it started being serialized in *Blackwood's Edinburgh Magazine,* he could count on a thorough familiarity with this type of fiction on the part of his readers.

The writer of quest fiction whom Blackburn is most obviously parodying is H. Rider Haggard, whose *King Solomon's Mines* (1885) had been succeeded by many dozen works by him on the same theme, and by hundreds of adventure romances by others from all over the colonial world. The Haggard school of romanticizing frontier expansionism and casting quests to the interior in allegorical frameworks was, of course, anathema to Blackburn. There is evidence that he held a figure like Haggard in irritated contempt.[6] Yet Haggard himself was a pioneer of value, of a previous generation of colonial writers. Haggard opened up the world of the frontier to an unprecedentedly large and avid readership. In works such as *She* (1887), and in the many other works that pursue the career of the South African hunter-adventurer, Allan Quatermain, he discovered a formula for the colonial adventure romance which is both persuasive and enduring. While Blackburn's work parodies Haggard, with a satirical energy and even a venom that is uniquely his own, *Richard Hartley, Prospector* could not exist without its forebears in the tradition.

What was familiar to readers of Haggard, then, was the structuring of a quest novel into three obvious areas of plot: (1) preparation, (2) the expedition into the interior, and (3) the triumphant return. In Haggard the preparatory phase is marshalled together in as few pages as possible, the expedition itself receives the main attention, and the return is often cursorily handled as a foregone conclusion. Haggard's stress, too, in handling this formula is on the ongoing impetus of the adventure, not on its motivation, implications, and consequences—action is all. Haggard lapses into the briefest, tight-lipped asides only when he wishes to slacken tension, or angle the direction of the action into a new phase. His work is enthrallingly packed with deeds performed by men who often have little facility with words, and it makes compulsive reading because the accumulation of deeds is skillfully patterned to conform to the basics of all quest literature. The faith of the questers through all hardships is ultimately rewarded by the discovery of the quest object, characters are tested and enriched by the rigors of life experience, and the whole is a reenactment of an old myth of discovery which was popular once more in the second half of the nineteenth century. As Britain's campaign of colonization took on the opening up of the remotest corners of the unknown world, bringing the fruits back to Europe, so Haggard prevailed as chronicler. But by 1899 the merry romps of Haggard's brainless fictions for younger readers had begun to appear naive and phoney. The romance of high imperialism was meeting the realism of a thoroughly modern, uncontainable, and cripplingly costly war.

That Haggard was Blackburn's target in *Richard Hartley, Prospector* can scarcely be doubted. The name Richard Hartley itself is a parodic version of the name Rider Haggard. Blackburn gave himself good reason for initiating this kind of private joke. It seems clear from a letter he wrote Blackwood's in June 1903 that he had been working on *Richard Hartley* for a long time: he asked George W. Blackwood if it would be wise:

to finish a novel I have had on the stocks for four years, dealing with the Rand before the Renaissance, and affording me an opportunity to use up the very large store of interesting personal experience I have had up in the country, ranging from quests for hidden treasure and lost tribes, prospecting, fighting Kafirs and hunting cattle thieves down to the less exciting events of Pretorian intrigue, financial & political. (*EiA*, 38)

This obviously refers to *Richard Hartley*, and so the early part of the composition of the work dates from Blackburn's Krugersdorp days.

In 1896, approximately at the time Blackburn was planning the composition of *Richard Hartley, Prospector*, he wrote an editorial in the *Transvaal Sentinel* which, in part, reads as follows:

To the frothy nonsense talked at the South African Writers' Dinner in London the other evening Mr Rider Haggard the fiction manufacturer contributed more than his share. In the ordinary course such drivel would not be worth a moment's consideration but unfortunately Mr Haggard is identified with South Africa, and an undiscriminating English public take it for granted that any man who has spent sufficient time in this country to be able to mis-spell a few stock native names and phrases is worth listening to as an oracle on any South African subject from the Scab Act to the quality of veldschoons in use in any particular district. (*TS*, July 19, 1896)

This is one of Blackburn's most scathing literary commentaries, and it seems to be aiming in many directions. First, it is Haggard's glib and superficial knowledge of the land—evidenced in the works by the inept details of local color with which they are besprinkled—which is under attack. For Blackburn it was increasingly to become a matter of pride that he took great pains to research his works exhaustively. Second, it is Haggard's jingoistic advocacy of the British cause in the Transvaal which Blackburn reviles:

Mr Haggard expressed his desire to see the English flag again floating at Pretoria where, said he, it used to be;[7] but he omitted to mention that the reason it no longer flaunts there is because the British Government proved itself utterly incompetent to do anything in the shape of governing beyond paying the salaries of idle ornamental officials of whom Mr Haggard was one. . . . Fortunately Mr Haggard's wishes are not likely to be realized, and he may console himself with the fact that by sticking to fiction he will earn his money with much more credit. . . . (*TS*, July 19, 1896)

Out of this tortuous political disagreement Blackburn proceeded to shape *Richard Hartley, Prospector.* Nor was Blackburn insensitive to changes of taste in the reading public, so that there is a second explanation for the shape that *Richard Hartley* takes. In the same letter to Blackwood's, he adds:

> I am quite alive to the fact that public opinion and taste are variable quantities, I am also old enough to have survived the optimistic enthusiasm that ignores the practical (I am in my 47th year). Therefore you need have no scruples as to hurting any vanity I may possess by talking with frankness, as I need scarcely remark your counsel on such matters would entirely influence any action, before I began it.

What Blackwood replied to Blackburn is not recorded, but evidently they took to Blackburn's own summary of *Richard Hartley,* and were sufficiently confident in it to serialize it as well as to publish it in book form. Presumably, then, Blackburn's aim was to sell them a work which while, in some respects, appeared to be yet another romance of the quest type, was also a realist novel that bears a distinctly odd and innovatory relationship to its predecessors.

The parody works at almost all levels of the novel. In the Haggard version the British expedition takes enlightenment into the interior, and its mission is to diffuse the civilizing process; in Blackburn the expedition carts weaponry inland which is as likely to be used against the white man as on his behalf. In Haggard the trio of the expedition—the members of which often correspond to a psychological model as superego, ego, and id, as if the team had one personality parcelled out into three beings—is interdependent and remains unassailably unified, exemplifying the unity of the British cause; in Blackburn the members of the trio are tied together by no ideals other than economic expediency, and their very composition is explosive. In Haggard there is a moral justness about the trip, and its rewards are described as fairly and legitimately earned, albeit often out of all proportion to their initial investments; in Blackburn it is never less than clear that their quest is plainly immoral, and the copious sums of money they raise are shown to be beyond all reason. Blackburn's allegory is, by contrast with Haggard's, sinister, even gruesome, and certainly condemns the exploitative nature of the entire quest exercise.

Wilmot himself is a character who has grown up on the Haggard type of African romance and so, inserting Wilmot into a latter-day version of the same old genre, Blackburn can show up its inadequacies. The Africa that Wilmot arrives in is by no means the untrammeled wilderness of Haggard's hinterland, either. When he has spent his small fortune and tried, but failed, to find work on the industrializing Rand, his inner resources run dry, and the novel begins with him at his wit's end. Blackburn is specific as to the reasons why:

> For the first time in his uneventful life of twenty-five years he had been brought face to face with the stern fact that he was a failure, superfluous and insignificant, and the little world of the Rand, which he came out with light heart to conquer, neither regarded nor wanted him. Ignorance and pride prevented his knowing that he was but a very ordinary type of a species too common on the Rand, as in most new countries. Bred to a life of inert ease, on the strength of expectations never fulfilled, he had found himself at five-and-twenty forced to earn his bread, yet totally unprovided with any special knowledge or fitness that would enable him to hold his own against the keen competitors in the struggle for life in great cities. Then came the too frequent sequel. It was decided by his friends that, having been a failure at home, he was precisely the kind of man a new and strenuous country like the Transvaal needed. . . .[8]

This is not the tone of the genre as we have come to expect it; rather, Blackburn is witheringly critical of his hero. In *Richard Hartley* we have the strange result that Wilmot makes his fortune in spite of himself, and then only thanks to the resourceful and practical Hartley. Wilmot's flight from the country when the going becomes rough is also the epitome of cowardice.

In short, Wilmot is one of Blackburn's stock characters—the naive pawn of chance whose actions never seem to correlate with his rewards, either in terms of financial gain or in terms of disabuse of his ideals. He is a far more acutely observed version of the antihero narrator of *Kruger's Secret Service,* and will come into his own in the guise of Sarel Erasmus, the narrator of a trilogy of novels.

In contrast, the real hero of the novel is Richard Hartley, a character whom Blackburn presents, without any great irony or debunking, as a rather unusual straight man. He is reliable, compassionate, intelligent, a patriot for South Africa (rather than a simple-minded British/Boer supporter), a man who blazed the mineral trail open for the miners and manufacturers to follow but who is, by the opening of the action of the novel, edged out of the very expansionism he has caused. With access neither to financial power in Johannesburg, nor to political power in Pretoria, he constantly shrinks from his destiny, being phased out into an inglorious end of drunken brawling and abject poverty. For Hartley the expedition, despite its dubious nature, is a means of pulling off a last gamble against the powers of fortune that have ruled his life to date. There is something splendidly hopeless about his individual daring, particularly since he fatalistically accepts that he probably will lose everything in the end. Hartley has a plodding, dogged strength, much given though he is to running out of words, tampering shyly with his pipe, and brooding bitterly.

What makes Hartley's part of the story moving and exceptional is that the adventure romancer—who would normally place the Wilmot character centrally and see to it that the younger man gained in the education of life—here puts a broken has-been into the focal role. Blackburn plays this big variation on our expectations of the genre by showing us that, even in this extreme case, a near-derelict can also be sobered and blistered by experience into a kind of new maturity. Hartley's fortunes do change in accordance with the social change that overtakes the Transvaal after the war—during the Renaissance to which Blackburn refers, which occurred after the 1902 peace treaty. But Blackburn seems to be working at the Hartley story in great detail to show even more: Hartley is, in the end, a true hero, not because he is able to come into his own by some foredestined right, but because when he is beset by an impossibly complicated experience, he can transcend himself and change fundamentally.

This could, perhaps, be ascribed to the power that Blackburn feels is the force of love. Yet the love scenes between Clarie and Hartley are handled abruptly, and none of it conforms to the undying, deathless variety that is usually the stuff of the adventure romance. For a start, it is situated differently in *Richard Hartley*. In the Haggard version, the hero's beloved is invariably located at Home, the base from which the novel proceeds and to which it returns. The Haggard hero remains inviolate, purely related to the beloved, whose hand he earns, as it were, through his pluck in proving himself an adequate provider. Then we have the reunion, marriage, fade-out. But in Blackburn's version of the myth, Hartley's beloved is placed on route as an obstacle in the course. His tentative, unconfident, shy love for her appears to be a handicap rather than an inspiration. Nor on his return with his spoils is the winning of her hand automatic; on the contrary, the climactic reversal of the novel is that she rejects him. In one scene Blackburn has Hartley so floundering with disappointment that he literally rides his horse into a quicksand (the same marshy patch, it turns out, that Jameson and his flying relief column bogged down in outside Krugersdorp a year before). So, Blackburn does not seal his novel with anything like the traditional, pat happy ending.

In fact, Blackburn extends the genre quite beyond what it usually carries. The double plots of the Wilmot story and the Hartley story, interwoven for the body of the work, also separate very unexpectedly. In the Wilmot case, Blackburn interpolates a peculiar episode which befalls Wilmot during his escape south. By accident he trespasses on the domain of a man without a name, a Britisher who has defected from a life of some standing in the United Kingdom to live out the rest of his days as a recluse beyond the frontier of British civilization. The recluse is a man of learning and a violinist, given to quoting Tennyson's "In Memoriam" from memory (the portrait is obviously reminiscent of Blackburn himself in his Loteni days). In this author's surrogate's company, Wilmot is obliged to work over all the details of his story; together the two of them sift through its meanings and its implications. It is altogether possible that had the war not intervened at the end of the four years Blackburn had already spent working on the novel, *Richard Hartley, Prospector* would have ended more conventionally. But as it now stands, completed and rounded off from Blackburn's own place of refuge from the war, we have a work which strangely begins to interrogate itself. The effect of this stock-taking is for it to stop being one kind of novel (the parody adventure) and to break into being an altogether more philosophical, revaluative meditation (the beginnings of the psychological, realist novel).

The recluse is a "tall, aesthetic-looking man in a pyjama suit and a broad panama hat" (*RHP,* 325), who has built himself a perfectly neat African-style household. He is known by the Zulus as the "man who can see through everything" (*RHP,* 328). To him, Wilmot confides the following: "Mine is a strange story . . . the sort of thing one reads about in fiction but rarely meets in real life" (*RHP,* 328), to which the recluse sagely replies: "Which is another way of saying your experience, whatever it may have been, is of a common South African type. Shall we say a story of phantom fortune, of greed and—and the consequences of greed?" (*RHP,* 328).

This process of distilling the patterns of experience, and the ability of literature to contain them, results in a parallel being drawn between Wilmot's story and that of the adventure hero who heads the whole gallery of British lone voyagers, Robinson Crusoe: "The boy reads *Robinson Crusoe* because of the thrill of adventure, and is a little disappointed because the savages don't attack oftener. The man sees in it a fascinating vindication of the triumph of action over adversity" (*RHP*, 335). But over this adventure novel for adults hangs a pall of disillusionment appropriate to the hermit figure of a Wordsworth or a Coleridge; our recluse has turned his back on civilization in favor of the pursuit of happiness in nature. He says of his God's little acre, "I don't know what the return per acre was from the Garden of Eden, but I don't think it would beat this valley" (*RHP*, 337). Of civilization itself he has this to remark: "If the ultimate aim of progress is happiness, it has failed miserably so far. . . . Until I am convinced by results that the civilised state is productive of the greatest happiness to the greatest number, I shall continue to believe that the Kafir is nearer the *summum bonum* than the white" (*RHP*, 341–42). This line of thought, which is quite alien to the adventure romance, sends Wilmot reeling from the recluse's presence, recovered in limb but destroyed in ideals. His exit from the novel suggests his ruin, and he goes without his share of the diamonds, too.

Hartley, meanwhile, works for some years in utter seclusion to come to similarly socialist and determinist conclusions about the nature of society, and the quest for happiness and personal fulfillment within society. When Hartley emerges from seclusion in the Drakensberg, the war is in its final stages. The old order changeth indeed (as one of the titles of the chapters reminds us). He receives a cutting from the *Transvaal Staats Courant,* "an official advertisement offering a reward of £250 for the apprehension of Richard Hartley and Graham Wilmot for the crime of high treason," to which Blackburn appends the remark: "Field cornets are instructed to apply for the reward at an office that has now ceased to exist" (*RHP*, 362).

Hartley is afforded a last opportunity of wiping the slate clean, of making a new beginning. His qualifications for this are unexceptionable; he speaks the Taal as well as he does English, he is honest to a fault about geological potential, and he is motivated to rebuild a more equitable world from the smouldering ruins of the old. When he reencounters Clarie in a concentration camp—most of her family has been wiped out and her old Voortrekker farm razed to the ground—they agree to marry, without sentimentality and for practical reasons. Their first kiss is made in a burial ground within the camp, where body upon body is dug in anonymously, bodies of soldiers, women, children, indiscriminately thrown together. The style of Blackburn's narration remains calmly detached, nonpartisan, what he accurately describes as "bald matter-of-fact" (*RHP*, 254). Through this he builds an immensely powerful groundswell of hope for a future over the "racial barrier" (*RHP*, 104), one of reconciliation between the two white races. With the marriage of Hartley and Clarie, *Richard Hartley, Prospector* becomes one of the first novels to resolve the Anglo-Boer conflict in this way. Hartley lives on, a new South African, investing his hard-earned takings back into the land that will nourish his and Clarie's children.

The ending of *Richard Hartley, Prospector* might appear to be merely a new twist to the old formula, sociologically caused by circumstances which overtook Blackburn during the writing. But it could well be maintained that Blackburn's novel ends at this point for a lot of other reasons. A fundamental tenet in Blackburn's technique throughout the work is to revise all notions that are stereotypical or merely formulaic. He systematically embroiders on the typologies of the older adventure romance to overturn and revise them. Nothing, in Blackburn's novel, is what it seems. The reader's every normal expectation is teased, played with, directed in a different course. This is true of the whole, but it also applies to the smallest details.

Here, for example, is a description of how our expectations of the hierarchy of Johannesburg social life are strangely scrambled by the real thing:

During his sojourn in Johannesburg [Wilmot] had met too many millionaires who looked like loafers, and loafers who suggested millionaires, to allow a man's appearance and manner to influence him. He had never forgotten that the illiterate bricklayer who shared his bedroom at the Imperial International Canteen, and had but one change of raiment, had a banking account running into four figures, and was the principal shareholder in a prosperous brick and tile business; nor that the billiard-marker at the Red Crown was a Bachelor of Arts of Cambridge, and the lady who supplied milk to the hotel the wife of a broken-down Scottish baronet of ancient lineage. . . . (*RHP*, 57–58)

In Pretoria, Wilmot's experience is similarly topsy-turvy. In the following passage Blackburn echoes the title of a work which he frequently praised as the beginning of the South African novel of urban realism, J. R. Couper's *Mixed Humanity*:[9]

> Pretoria, always interesting to English visitors during the Kruger *régime*, was doubly absorbing at this period. Boerdom was revelling in its apotheosis. The excitement attendant on the abortive Reform movement and the Jameson Raid has hardly begun to cool down. The Reformers were still in jail, and the capital was a centre of interest for half the civilised world. Never before had it been so full of mixed humanity. Field cornets from remote districts, who had never till now seen the Mecca of Boer officialdom, sympathetic representatives of the sister Free State and Cape Colony, German concession-hunters, seeking the reward of the loyalty of their country to the threatened but triumphant Republic, newspaper "specials," globe-trotters, and a crowd of friends of the incarcerated revolutionists, swarmed in the hotels and public places, giving to life in the town a bustle and vitality that contrasted strangely with Wilmot's preconceived notions of the sleepy Boer capital, as derived from many a book of travellers' immatured impressions. (*RHP*, 136)

Wilmot and the reader are, in this way, privileged to a behind-the-scenes view. In due course Wilmot is jailed in Pretoria for a somewhat lengthy sojourn. Out of sheer boredom he attends a flogging of a "Kaffir" which makes him sick and faint, but in no way changes his attitudes to the justice meted out to black prisoners. This, however, is the main subject of Blackburn's later novel, *Leaven*, which is *Richard Hartley*'s natural successor.

Black characters make scant appearances in *Richard Hartley, Prospector*, and then only as fellow workers and servants. The only black character who fits into the category of "noble savage"—the category which Haggard enlarged to include whole mythical inland empires, like that of Monomatapa, for which the Rhodesia of the time would be an analogue—is called Bulalie, and we can spare a smile at the fact that he is named after one of Haggard's heroes.[10]

Although there is much in *Richard Hartley, Prospector* that is finely achieved and of provocative interest, there can also be no doubt that it is an overdone piece of work, not thought through to the last detail, a process which might have turned it from an interesting landmark into a masterpiece. The first half of the novel sprawls somewhat gratuitously, as Blackburn strains to enmesh all the texture and times of Johannesburg and Pretoria and the surrounding country. So concerned is he to report on it all that he tends to slacken his focus on character development for the sake of accumulation of data. Admittedly, the minutiae of observation and the wonderfully accurate beauty of the social environment is breathtakingly done, a pleasure in its own right. But *Richard Hartley, Prospector* strains at the seams; where its predecessors cut all corners in order to further the plot, in this work the plot is overburdened with impedimenta. It is a fascinating and utterly convincing expose of the world Blackburn knew so well (and perhaps we should not ask for more), but perhaps, in all the years of its composition (1897–1903), it grew out of hand, too bulky for its initial, brilliant idea. Certainly *Kruger's Secret Service* is a more potent work, for what it leaves out, than *Richard Hartley, Prospector.*

Critical opinion about *Richard Hartley* in South Africa, although thoroughly appreciative, had much the same point to make. It is interesting to note that Blackburn was widely held by those in the know—the Transvalers themselves—to be an exemplary and fair commentator on their scene. Thus the critic of the *Star,* the paper for which Blackburn had reported a decade before:

The man's a trained writer—it can be seen with half an eye—and he knows the technique of his trade. What is more, he has the gift of quick observation and the gift of sharp description. His scallywags of the reef and the veld and also the more respectable people to whom he occasionally introduces us, are drawn with those quick and telling touches which make fiction more life-like than a photograph. Therefore, when Mr Blackburn devotes himself to characterisation he succeeds as admirably as he did in *Prinsloo of Prinsloosdorp.* But when he comes to attempt a sustained plot, his strength or this assiduity seems to fail, and the story drags and wanders. So does *Richard Hartley.*[11]

Nevertheless, the reviewer concludes, giving us a fair indication of the norms of criticism in Blackburn's day and of his reputation: "like Mr Blackburn's other books, it is in a different class to anything else in the way of South African story-writing since Olive Schreiner's early work."

Chapter Three
The Sarel Erasmus Satires

Douglas Blackburn's major creative energy went into his most acclaimed project as a novelist—if his writing deserves to be remembered, certainly his Sarel Erasmus trilogy of satires must stand as his finest achievement.

The trilogy was not planned as such; rather, it happened book by book across a decade. It stretches from *Prinsloo of Prinsloosdorp,* completed by 1897 and first published in 1899, through *A Burgher Quixote,* written in 1900–1902 and published in 1903, and concludes with *I Came and Saw,* written in 1906–7 and published in 1908. But the three works are united by their common narrator, Sarel Erasmus, a fictional Boer character whose style Blackburn used like a ventriloquist his dummy. Sarel not only grows and flourishes through the sequence, but requires his readers to keep in step with him as an author of increasing stature and notoriety. Never in South African literature has the use of a mouthpiece like this been sustained for so long, nor displayed such a panoply of ongoing historical events.

While the Sarel Erasmus works appeared at intervals throughout Blackburn's career—interspersed with other novels of a different nature—it is appropriate to group them together in one chapter, the liveliest and most accomplished chapter of Blackburn's life.

Prinsloo of Prinsloosdorp

Blackburn's novella, *Prinsloo of Prinsloosdorp,* has Piet Prinsloo as its eponymous hero. The narration spans sixty years of his life, between his teens in the Cape Colony and young adulthood as a transport rider on the Kimberley diamond fields, through to his maturity in the Transvaal, and ends with his evacuation to Rhodesia in the middle of the 1890s. The saga of the Prinsloo dynasty is a sequence of such speedy evacuations, beginning in the seventeenth century from France when the Edict of Nantes was "served upon

Jacobus Piet Prinsloo the Huguenot, compelling him to *trek* to South Africa."[1] In South Africa, ever since, "wherever there has been action, civil or martial, there was a Prinsloo to be found" (*PP*, 1). In short, Piet Prinsloo is an exemplar of Boer history in the nineteenth century.

His is a life lived in contentious strife with the British: The birth of Piet was attended by circumstances of sadness and depression. He was the thirteenth child by the third wife of that Hans Prinsloo who led the Burghers against the English tax collector whom they justly killed at Oliphant's Kloof. The year of Piet's birth (1835) was the one wickedly chosen by the British Government for the ruin of the Colonials by freeing their slaves. (*PP*, 2)

These two issues—the compelling of Boer communities to compete in the British colonial economy through the paying of cash taxes, and the removal of their reservoirs of cheap labor through the abolition of slavery—cause their next trek, this time over the border at the Orange River, an event which is, in fact, the central migration of orthodox South African historians, the epic Great Trek. In Blackburn's version of the saga, nothing may be taken as particularly heroic or clear-cut.

On the second page of his satirical history, he begins to weave in several other causes of this cross-continental removal, chief of which is the Prinsloos' understandable desire to avoid crookery and double-dealing:

Hans Prinsloo owned many slaves, and according to the rate of compensation awarded, he should have received £600. But the Government, instead of paying in honest gold, did what all Englanders are fond of doing to this day: they gave the owners pieces of paper called "Treasury Bills," payable in London. Now, it was foolishness to expect poor Boers to travel to England, of which they knew nothing, and cash those bills, so they fell victim to the rascally Englanders who went round the country offering to go to London and collect the money. Hans Prinsloo was deceived by one of these *Rooineks*, who told him that the English Government had no more money, which was why they paid in paper. He so frightened him that Hans sold him the bill for £20. (*PP*, 2)

This financial detail, which is used tellingly through the work, here illustrates the extent of the fraud perpetrated on the gullible Boers, and we can accept the resulting circumstances with sympathy:

Thus it was that when Piet came into the world he found his family so poor that they had to farm with hired Kaffirs and even had sometimes to work themselves. Little wonder that the name of Englander was hated by him all the days of his life, and that he distrusted all kinds of written papers. (*PP*, 3)

Here we have several complications to what is often presented as a simple story; Blackburn is intent on revealing a set of real motives beside a set of pretended ones. In being forced to hire labor, the Prinsloos fail to keep up financially in the post-abolition economy, and furthermore are unable to indulge in their ideal of slothfully lording it over a captive work force.

Another factor which renders them ill-equipped to deal with the intrusions of British life is their inefficiency over matters of literacy and accounting, which puts them at the butt-end of every second incident in the work. As a result, Piet's own necessary talent for double-dealing is nurtured early on, and he becomes an avid learner in the techniques of deception. But he is offered a chance of acquiring the skills with which to survive legitimately:

For a short time Piet was taught at a farm school by an old German teacher whom he hated, because he pressed him to learn cyphering. But the schooling did not last long, for one day Piet finished the master, though no one knew how it happened. It came about this way. Piet and the old German were riding to a distant farm when they had to cross a river in flood. The old man could not see well and had to ask Piet which were the bad places in the ford. Piet showed him a place where the current was deep and strong and the teacher was carried away, so there was no more schooling. (*PP*, 3–4)

Piet's resistance to acculturation with the rudiments of an education beyond the Bible is, it appears, casually smart, but his murdering of one unfortunate wandering "meester" is hardly a solution to his dilemma. Indeed, Piet frequently comes to realize his foolishness:

In after days Piet often regretted that he had done this thing, for, said he:
"Had I been able to cypher and read writing as the old teacher wished, I should not have been *verneuked* by so many *Rooineks.*" (*PP*, 4)

The real point is that had Piet been literate in words and figures he would have been able to learn to fend for himself in the urban centers. But his reaction, instead of overcoming his disabilities, is to trek beyond the frontier to a newer world where he can evade both the realities of the developing land, no longer in his power, and the consequences of his malicious actions. Piet's is a rearguard, loser's defense, and he is really in love with his own freedom. In order to keep uninvaded, Piet translates his world into one populated with knaves, the British chief among them. His own vulnerability causes his defensiveness. His very insistence on the universal prevalence of roguery becomes a mania with him and the central justification for his own greatest ambition, to become a greater rogue than anyone else. While Piet will consistently maintain that he is a simple "son of the soil" and one of the true patriots of his days, his real self is as rascally as he can devise: outscheming, outplotting, and outwitting a hostile world become his way of self-preservation. His mission to avenge the crookery over the Treasury bills becomes his excuse for increasingly immoral, irreligious, and illegal actions. His own redeeming virtue, if indeed it is one, is his inventive cunningness at keeping one step ahead of the law, be it the law of the Cape, of the Free State, or of the Zuid-Afrikaansche Republiek or Transvaal. This undeveloped pastoral backwater—unsurveyed, and a refuge for agricultural berserkers—is evidently the natural playground for Piet Prinsloo, and the story of Piet and his roguish schemes is also the story of the Transvaal up to the war.

This "biography" of Piet Prinsloo is recounted by his son-in-law, Sarel Erasmus, and the novella is his first work. Being of a new generation, Sarel has at least learned to read and write. His literary pretensions are few; his purpose is merely to vindicate the "character of a father of his country and founder of the *dorp* that bears his name" (PP, v). There are few details in this work about Sarel himself, except that he is married to one of Piet's unnumbered offspring. By a process of nepotism, he tags along enjoying the fruits of Piet's progress. Sarel's vindication is rendered faithfully, for the voice of Piet Prinsloo is maintained in indirect speech for lengthy passages. As Sarel never fully interprets Piet's story, but merely records it, we may also assume that he endorses his father-in-law's story and has no great ability to learn from it or alter his attitudes as a result. By maintaining his peace, in fact, he has benefited greatly from Piet's crooked dealings, and his own sense of outrage at the injustices committed against his adoptive family make him the novelist's ideal naive mouthpiece. Owing to the "respect which we Afrikanders bear for our seniors" (*PP*, v), Sarel is compelled to nurse his own grievances in favor of setting the record straight in respect of theirs. His intention in writing the life which the novella comprises is "to shame [Piet's] detractors by telling the truth as far as in me lies" (*PP*, vii).

Sarel, then, despite Blackburn's pun on the word "lies," is no mendacious crook. He is quite sincere when he writes: "How often do we read stories told in derision of the Boer which should only be told to his honor?" (*PP*, ix). Indeed, the peculiar twists and turns of the narrative reveal as much understanding of the Prinsloos as they do censure. The essence of the satire lies in the balance between sympathy and censure, for, while Sarel elaborates his apology, the elements of mitigation and condemnation accumulate about equally. Blackburn's technique is to let the reader see through and beyond the transparency of Sarel's view of the situation, and to experience to the full extent the complexity of the dilemmas which bring it about. The reader is privileged to follow Sarel's view, a partial, linear one, and at the same time to follow the cause and effect of the circumstances which Sarel himself is ill-equipped to notice. Sarel himself is a simpleton, unable to see beyond the stereotypes and ideals on which his world operates, and all the more winning for that.

To achieve this satirical effect, Blackburn uses an uncomplicated style, rendering the story in the English Sarel might well have used. It is unadorned with any literary affectation or trick of rhetoric. His very directness is a testament to his supposed honesty and straightforwardness. Blackburn also has Sarel's English—which is his second language after Dutch-Afrikaans—finely attuned to a blend of expression which is common in the Transvaal to this day. Sarel's syntactical errors reflect the influence of the word order and idioms of the Taal. A few examples are the inversions in "And it was so done" (*PP*, 124) and "Hans Breda had the getting of it up" (*PP*, 122), and the adjective "rejoiceful" (*PP*, 121). He has occasional recourse to biblical quotation which in the English translation from the High Dutch often sounds incongruous. For example, we have Piet's last quoted line: "We can sell them our transport cattle and our forage, and so spoil the Egyptians by getting their gold" (*PP*, 129), Egyptians being Englanders in this case.

Where Sarel cannot find English equivalents for South African concepts, he uses the word or phrase from the Taal italicized, which compels the glossary at the beginning of the work. But here, unlike other writers on Boer subjects, Blackburn is not merely sprinkling his fiction with words from Afrikaans to lend it local color, but exploring the technically untranslatable. Sarel finds the English for *schelm* ("rascal"), *sjambok* ("rawhide whip"), *slim* (which Blackburn renders as "tricky"), *tronk* ("jail"), and *verneukery* ("low cheating") flavorless and without impact. These verbal signs serve to characterize Sarel and his homespun world view with precision and uniqueness, and to anyone in the know the work sounds quite authentic.

Piet escapes into the Transvaal in the 1860s, and the body of *Prinsloo* contains further elaborated episodes on the above themes, similar in type but with increasingly dense implications. The following key historical events play out in the background: the unification of the Transvaal as the Z.A.R. with the assumption of Pretoria as its capital; the establishment of the Volksraad with its grondwet or constitution; the Zulu Wars of 1879–80 over the Natal border; the annexation of the Transvaal by the Haggard gang; the Boers' Declaration of Independence at Paardekraal and the battles of Laing's Nek and Majuba which constitute the First Anglo-Boer War; the arrival of the gold rush, proclamation of gold fields and the foundation of Johannesburg; the last punitive commando expeditions against independent black chiefs like Magato and, finally, the election by which Kruger retains the presidency from Piet Joubert just prior to the Jameson Raid.

Yet Piet's role in all this cavalcade of history is not really an eyewitness one; in fact, he spends most of his career avoiding the issues of the day, in favor of profiting from them at a safe distance. Despite his badge of patriotism and righteousness, Piet is a dodger. While the pivotal events of the period pass him by, he leads a life of playing for his personal advantage. The steps of his elevation are taken in this order: marriage, a landdrostship or magistracy (to which Sarel plays public prosecutor), field cornet and collector of customs (to which Sarel plays postmaster), storekeeper, farmer and founder of a proclaimed gold field complete with town. Along the way he makes sallies into black labor recruitment and cattle rustling as well. His greatest bid is to gain a seat in the Volksraad, but he is caught out on a minor bookkeeping infringement and treks on to Rhodesia, where, an exceedingly wealthy man, he dies of dropsy.

The result of this approach of Blackburn's to the story of the Transvaal is that we have a personalized, behind-the-scenes history which reveals in fiction all the secrets of the workings of the republic as they affected the average citizen. Blackburn would chronicle the same again later in a more reportorial way in *Secret Service in South Africa*.

Like *Kruger's Secret Service*, *Prinsloo of Prinsloosdorp* was also first published anonymously. When it was reprinted for the third time in 1908—for the first time with Blackburn's name attached as the author—he acknowledged in his preface to the new edition the controversial and flattering reception the work had received at various times, but somewhat modestly defined the author's role in it as follows: "He has merely collected a bunch of representative flowers of the Veld. All that he can legitimately claim as his own are the method of arrangement and the thread that binds them together" (preface [1908], xii). In later novels Blackburn would learn to work folk material into more intricate and organic structures, but here we feel he is assessing his achievement in *Prinsloo* rather accurately. His evaluation of it as a "bunch" of tales "collected" together is fair, as the work is indeed a sequence of often tenuously connected fragments. The "thread" that binds them together is also often unclear or without direction, so that the final effect of *Prinsloo* is, indeed, that of an anthology of favorite Transvaal tales about stupidity and revenge, about chicanery and corruption, about smartness and opportunism, and, above all, about hypocrisy and the abuse of true patriotism—an anthology that any reader on the spot would have relished for its canny, wild humor alone.

Thus, *Prinsloo of Prinsloosdorp* is not a tale written with any simple or self-evident morality. The reader is as much moved by Piet's vulnerability as angered by his adoption of corrupt ways, as much amused by his education in knavery as appalled by the casual violence toward, and exploitation of, those weaker than himself. And the true schlemiels of *Prinsloo* are not the Boers but the ultragullible blacks, dispossessed by taxes, herded into recruitment camps, and reduced to labor units in the background, expendable counters that permit the action, while all their exploiters gaze skywards with hands raised toward a deluge of Kruger pounds (the cover of the 1908 edition depicts Z.A.R. coins pelting from the sky). If Piet stands indicted of opportunism and greed, so does the entire system which encourages these qualities upon him as the norm and not the exception. Most important of all, the work insists that we understand the whole complexity of the reasons why.

The Sarel Erasmus Satires

This is a profoundly different achievement from that of the "globe trotters" Blackburn mentions in his preface of 1908, the writers with their superficial, prejudiced portraits. *Prinsloo* is indeed the first attempt in South African fiction to discuss the Boer and his burgeoning society in the Transvaal from within. Significantly, Blackburn did not break cover on his authorship of *Prinsloo* until after the war, and to this day it appears indexed in some public library collections (for example, the State Library in Pretoria and the British Library in London) as a work of fact by one Sarel Erasmus. The necessary hints are dropped in the first edition for the skilled reader to penetrate this camouflage pretty quickly, but as the themes of literacy and of misreading are so prevalent in the text we may assume that for many it worked as a genuine document.

Its impact would have been equivalent, if slightly more glorified, to that of an anonymous pamphlet—a form with which Blackburn was familiar enough—and of the allied forms of the editorial leader and the open letter. That these journalistic forms should coalesce into the form of the biographical or memoir novella is not surprising for Blackburn, given the time and the place. Much of the ragged structuring and loose-endedness of *Prinsloo of Prinsloosdorp* may be attributed to its being a work of this nature in a transitional form. It makes sense, too, that the rise of the essentially middle-class urban form of the novel in the Transvaal coincides with the expansion of a city like Johannesburg, and that Sarel Erasmus moves into town with its printing presses to become an urban writer. A fruitful comparison here in terms of background and form could be made with Cervantes, one of Blackburn's favorite satirists, who likewise evolved picaresque novellas to mirror the citification of sixteenth-century Spain. This parallel has been drawn in the case of his next work, *Kruger's Secret Service;* in the sequel to *Prinsloo, A Burgher Quixote,* it is specifically exploited.

Reaction to *Prinsloo of Prinsloosdorp* in South Africa and in England was hardly neutral. Probably no single work since Schreiner's *The Story of an African Farm* of 1883 received as much coverage. The publishing history of *Prinsloo* attests to its success in terms of circulation both overseas and on its own home ground. The first of four editions of *Prinsloo* that appeared in Blackburn's lifetime is undated. Its composition must at least partly have postdated the passage of the New Press Law (September 1896) and, as in the writing of *Richard Hartley, Prospector,* Blackburn was probably overtaken by events as he attempted to finish it—this would explain the tacked on ending of *Prinsloo*. As Blackburn wrote in a letter of 1908 to Blackwood's, he sold the manuscript of *Prinsloo* outright to Dunbar Bros., probably when a Mr. Dunbar visited Krugersdorp to take photographs of local worthies, Blackburn among them, in June 1897.

The novella first appered as *Prinsloo of Prinsloosdorp: A Tale of Transvaal Officialdom, Being Incidents in the Life of a Transvaal Official, As Told to his Son-in-Law, Sarel Erasmus, Late Public Prosecutor of Prinsloosdorp, Market Master at Kaalkop, Small-pox Tax Collector of Schoonspruit, etc., etc.* in 1899, as a 129-page octavo hardback at 3s. 6d., with a green cover embossed with a gold engraving of an ox wagon on trek. (The date of deposition of this green original edition in the British Library is April 18, 1899.) This edition contains an unsigned author's note, Sarel's forewords [*sic*], and the novella. It was printed in Britain and published by Dunbar Bros. from Chancery Lane and from their Johannesburg office in the Arcade Buildings, corner of President and Rissik Streets. Later in the year, the distribution of books published by Dunbar Bros. was taken over by H. MacLeay of Arundel Street, Strand, who later in 1899 reissued *Prinsloo* as part of their South African Series, in a blue edition, both in hardback and paperback. These editions were printed from the same plates, but with some differences in the decorative chapter headings, plus they contained full-page advertisements on previously blank pages of MacLeay's mining directories and souvenir books of South Africa.

The first printing to bear Blackburn's name—and the fourth edition—is a reset yellow and black paperback, published by Alston Rivers at one shilling, with the preface to the new edition, dated April 1908, in which Blackburn reviews the changes in the Transvaal over the decade since the work's first appearance. All these editions received press coverage in various lights.

The first major review of *Prinsloo of Prinsloosdorp*—one which served to a great extent to launch Blackburn's career as a novelist after the war—appeared anonymously in the *Spectator*, London, in 1899, when, as the editorial matter of that issue has it, the world was "trembling for news of Kruger's next move." Entitled "A South African Satirist," this notice runs to an amazing 225 lines, including substantial quotes, and begins thus:

The Sarel Erasmus Satires

A new satirist has arisen, and, appropriately enough, from Africa, the home of surprises. The anonymous author of *Prinsloo of Prinsloosdorp*, a true disciple of Swift, has not only levelled a trenchant indictment against Transvaal officialdom, but he has given us within the compass of a hundred and thirty pages as brilliant and sustained an essay in political irony as we can remember to have appeared in the last thirty years. . . .[2]

It is heralded as "a first rate work of art, which deserves a permanent place amid the literature of social and political satire."

Where the *Spectator* reviewer leaves the focus of the satire on the "ordinary Boer official," Blackburn's target is really the Pretoria government that tacitly sanctions his abuses. In the only incident in the work in which Piet beards Oom Paul Kruger himself in Pretoria, the president does not rebuke him for crookedness and bad faith, but calls him "a great fool, and said he was his stupidest Landdrost, for he was always getting the State into the papers" (*PP*, 69). Blackburn levels his final indictment at the state itself, not at the state's hapless, underpaid functionaries.

A second point, perhaps the most crucial in the work, is remarked upon by the *Spectator* reviewer but, with the war weeks away, cunningly sidestepped: "The frauds and acts of peculation of which Piet is guilty," the reviewer concludes, "are dwarfed into insignificance by the superior subtlety and audacity of 'Scotty,' the horse thief; of Brown, the millionaire . . . all of them Outlanders. This, however, is hardly the place to attempt to solve the political equation of the book."

The book itself does solve the equation: little fish in a sea of iniquity are eaten by bigger fish, which are eaten in turn by the real sharks; individual is devoured by state, which is itself devoured:

> Rotten—it is the only word to apply to South African society in the days when it was in the melting pot. Rotten—socially and morally, a land which never produced anything but gold and sordid-minded plutocrats.
> Rotten—and they say that, now, putrefaction has set in. I, for one, believe that to be true, and I advise those who do not believe, those who have faith in the much-vaunted New Era [of Union in 1910], to read Douglas Blackburn's book, and then see if they can imagine a social system which was infected by such poisonous germs at the outset ever growing strong enough to throw off the infection. . . .[3]

This retrospective opinion from the novelist Stanley Portal Hyatt (published in review of, and referring to, not *Prinsloo*, but *Secret*

Service in South Africa) stands as a somewhat emotional testament to the powerful effect Blackburn could have as an independent social commentator, with his panoptic vision and sense of causality in the history of South Africa.

Some reviewers within South Africa were fully able to duck the impact of *Prinsloo*. It is "authoritative" judgments like the following which contribute to the process whereby the point of Blackburn's achievement was gradually watered down and turned around to fall into line with the official views of the establishment. This is the entry on *Prinsloo* in Sidney Mendelssohn's *South African Bibliography*, the monumental work which summarizes and evaluates all of the literary development of South Africa up to 1910:

An amusing sketch representing the lower class of Burgher officials, in the person of a fictitious Boer Landrost. Although Piet Prinsloo was probably an exaggerated type, there can be no doubt that such men were employed by the government of the Transvaal Republic, and the author would appear to have touched up on many well-known abuses which were committed by these rustic legislators. The means by which these men, as well as others in higher positions, amassed considerable fortunes, are caustically exposed, and from the standpoint of the writer, there appeared to have been little scruple on the part of these officials in fleecing the Uitlanders, or robbing their own government. Many of the traits of the lower order of Boers are reproduced, together with interesting examples of their method of thought in justification of their actions; and from time to time real names of well-known men are brought into the narrative.

Comic fiction of profoundly subtle implications is here being disclassed before our eyes. The "well-known men," whom Blackburn makes a point of implicating—men like Kruger and Rhodes—are here screened out so that the central issue of the work, the conflict between rural socialist and urban capitalist systems, is defused. Thanks to critics like Mendelssohn, *Prinsloo* has been adjudged a mere curiosity (an ungenerous and spiteful one at that), and in time tended to be overlooked.

There is, nevertheless, a legendary aspect of the *Prinsloo* story which clings on in South Africa to this day, legendary in that it seems unverifiable in newspaper and archival sources. The story was doubtless spread by Blackburn himself to fan the flames of the gossip *Prinsloo* caused on its first appearance. It is the oft-repeated story that Kruger suppressed the work on its publication in the Transvaal by "wast[ing] public money in buying up an edition" (preface [1908], xii). Even a critic like Jack Cope in 1974 repeats this anecdote, though he incorrectly deduces from it that *Prinsloo* "falls outside the real tradition [of South African satire] because it is racially one-sided, being an English jape at the expense of the Afrikaners. . . ."[4] The burning of whole editions of *Prinsloos* might have been a story for Blackburn to dine out on, but judging by the quantities of the book still in circulation in South Africa today, any attempts to limit its sales were unsuccessful.

Prinsloo of Prinsloosdorp and its sequel, *A Burgher Quixote,* at least earned Blackburn a considerable literary reputation at the time. Hyatt himself called Blackburn "the father of the modern school of South African novelists,"[5] and in a post-Union survey like Sarah Gertrude Millin's "The South Africa of Fiction" *Prinsloo* is given very fair space:

so absurd and humorous a record of Boer slimness and naivete that it can produce nothing more than a flicker of amusement over the face of the sternest Dutchman. Its very exaggeration is disarming. For a satire is not a panegyric. And a caricature is, *ipso facto,* a libel. On the other hand, a perversion of the truth cannot but have truth as the basis of its inception. Now, therefore, if you wish to consider the career of the "slim kerel," Piet Prinsloo, as set forth in innocent protest by his virtue-loving son-in-law, you must do so in the light of these three axioms.[6]

Millin's suggested procedure for analyzing *Prinsloo* has not been followed in South African literary criticism, and the field is generally bare of any study of satire in the context of its times.

What was Blackburn's own attitude to the fiction he created in the last days of the Burgher Republic? There is only one comment of his on record. He puts his case in reply to an article of 1906 by John Forrest, in which Forrest surveyed fiction up to that date,[7] but in which, while praising *A Burgher Quixote* and *Richard Hartley, Prospector,* Forrest omitted all reference to *Prinsloo of Prinsloosdorp.* The number of February 1907 carries this cryptic note, signed by "Sojourner," and it is easy to suspect that "Sojourner" was Blackburn himself:

a correspondent reminds us that *Prinsloo of Prinsloosdorp,* by Douglas Blackburn, is well known at home and valued as a gently satirical picture of Transvaal life under "Oom Paul." . . . We agree with the statement that

Blackburn's aim is evidently "to sketch for a younger generation details of a past or passing phase of South African life, rather than to write fiction, the result being an inside view of historical happenings, very useful to relieve and illustrate the real South African history such as Dr Theal's."

We may take this view as definitive.

In 1978 *Prinsloo of Prinsloosdorp* was reissued in South Africa by the South African Universities Press of Cape Town in a facsimile reprint of the Rivers paperback, identical in all respects but the cover, and containing a new foreword by the publisher, W. P. du Plessis. At the time, not only was Blackburn's work going out of copyright and into the public domain, but the country was absorbed in the coils of a scandal that revealed a string of unholy corruptions in high places. Like the Watergate scandal that toppled President Richard Nixon, South Africa's Info Scandal forced Premier John Vorster to resign. The parallels between South Africa in the 1890s and in the 1970s did not go unremarked on in the reviews of the day. Sarah Christie noted a sense of déjà vu about *Prinsloo*[8] and John Grogan commended it as "one of the funniest [books] ever written in South Africa" as a result.[9] In the *Sunday Times* (Johannesburg) Ken Owen reproduced several apposite paragraphs of the work which needed no further commentary beyond the remark, "Timely reading."[10] And in an article Stanley Ridge gave *Prinsloo* a poignant accolade: "Its major importance for us is neither political nor documentary: Blackburn's devastating and yet compassionate humor was what was new, and it established certain possibilities for more conscious artists, particularly Herman Charles Bosman. . . ."[11]

What *Prinsloo of Prinsloosdorp* also did for Blackburn and for Sarel Erasmus was to open the way for their masterpiece, the finely achieved *A Burgher Quixote,* which, alas, is currently thoroughly out of print, and forgotten.

A Burgher Quixote

When in mid-1903 Blackwood's of Edinburgh published Blackburn's *A Burgher Quixote,* the memory of *Prinsloo of Prinsloosdorp* was still fresh. Reviewers of the former referred to the latter, and remarked on the continuity of the two works. But in *A Burgher Quixote* Blackburn moves his narrator forward; this large novel is very much Sarel Erasmus's own. Piet Prinsloo, the earlier subject, fades into the distance and is mentioned by Sarel only in passing a few times.

The Sarel Erasmus Satires

What carries over from *Prinsloo* is Sarel's own underplayed character, which now receives full, detailed, careful attention. And Blackburn's portrait of Sarel Erasmus is the most complex and sustained piece of characterization he ever attempted.

The plot of *A Burgher Quixote*, like all of Blackburn's plots, is intricate, and it compounds with great momentum. For this reason, it is no easy matter to summarize it fairly. The work itself moves forward on so many intertwining levels that we are truly damaging a finely balanced construct if we try and reduce it to its outline. However, the plot hinges on Sarel's dual allegiance to the Transvaal Republic and his "late countrymen," as he persistently calls them, and to the British flag. This split of interests is tested by experience in the crucible of the last months of 1899, with the outbreak of the Second Anglo-Boer War, and in the pitched battles of early 1900. The action of the novel peters out just as the action of the war petered out, once the first phase was over and a British victory was ensured. The date of completion of the work—approximately mid-1901—coincides with the results of the war, which had another year to run, being a foregone conclusion.

So, the action of *A Burgher Quixote* is narrowly confined to the few months in which Kruger's Z.A.R. committed itself to the gamble of a war campaign in which advances and reversals followed in rapid and dramatic succession. Sarel Erasmus is accordingly buffeted to and fro, but, characteristically, in a fashion which is so unorthodox and so unexpected that his account of his misadventures constitutes one of the funniest, and also the most poignant, records of those crucial events.

In 1898 or thereabouts, it happens that Sarel Erasmus left Prinsloosdorp, at the same time as his father-in-law trekked on, and our inexperienced young man joined a cousin on a farm over the border in Natal. He was evading two issues, the implications of which never cease to plague his attempts to make a fresh start. First, as public prosecutor and law agent of Prinsloosdorp he had defrauded the Transvaal government of some one thousand pounds. Second, he had betrothed himself to a large Boer woman named Katrina, making the mistake of borrowing from her a further thousand pounds, which he invests in Natal in cattle. (There is an inconsistency of plot here. In *A Burgher Quixote* Sarel has forgotten that he was married to Piet Prinsloo's daughter—the mistake is Blackburn's.) His move to Natal, then, was to get beyond the reach of both the law and his intended. The action of the novel actually opens with Sarel being called upon to return to Prinsloosdorp to defend a cousin in an obscure legal matter, and the call of blood must be obeyed. On his return Kruger's ultimatum and the declaration of war occur, and Sarel is trapped.

In Prinsloosdorp his debt to the state and his commitment to Katrina are both used as blackmail against him. Crooking the government is considered a normal peccadillo, but Sarel has to prove that it implies no disloyalty to the state by volunteering to fight for it. The aggressive Katrina is particularly patriotic and, like an avenging angel, insists that her man should bleed and die, like a true son of the soil, for the cause. Sarel, meanwhile, we gather, thanks to his stay in Natal and the widening of his horizons due to the allurements of a more modern world, has developed certain British sympathies, and abhors the idea of being sent to the firing line to shoot at the enemy whom he now construes as his friends. Thus, every subsequent action that he takes is devised specifically to avoid a confrontation situation. At the same time he has to make sufficient money to get himself off his double hooks. His dilemma is an excruciating one, aggravated by the rapid reversals of fortune of the war itself, and by the mistakes he makes that inevitably lead him deeper and deeper into a position where he will have to make a final decision about which side he means to join. To say that Sarel Erasmus is a torn man would be an understatement, and his constantly recurring "internal complaints" are understandable.

During the action Sarel himself is twice brought to trial, once by his own side, and then at the conclusion of the work by the British, on both occasions for having sympathies with the other side. In the first instance he is released and even promoted by the Burghers, having proved his fidelity, and in the second he is sentenced to lengthy imprisonment as a turncoat. The first trial, presided over by General Piet Joubert and Commandant Ben Viljoen—the actual historical personages—is precipitated by some minor prejudice against Sarel that brings the Boer commandoes near to hysteria in their vengefulness against him—as quartermaster at the front he is accused of poisoning a stock of looted whisky which has rendered the entire manpower of Boer troops incapable for a considerable period. Sarel the ex-prosecutor defends himself so ably that he is entrusted with recruiting his own commando. This is an irregular force of roughnecks, gangsters, and charlatans—the dregs

The Sarel Erasmus Satires

of the Boer volunteers—whom cunning Piet Joubert feels would be better used out of the battlefield on raiding expeditions into Natal. In short, Sarel becomes the unwilling head of a terrorist band whose only low motivation to fight is the quest for enemy loot. In the end, Sarel's ragged band deserts even him, and our Burgher Quixote is left in battle conditions without an army to lead. But in the few weeks that they are operative, this cluster of wild men do manage to exercise a brilliant and damaging campaign. It takes Sarel all the cunning he can devise to avoid having to loot his own farm on the other side, however.

The main action of Sarel's commando is caused by one of the key figures of the novel, Andries Brink, a fence-sitting schemer who literally makes a living between the battle lines, trading off both sides to his own advantage. A confidence man and a master of disguise (and of conjuring, Blackburn's old hobby), Brink is modeled on the historical renegade, "Scotty" Smith, frequently cited in the narrative and whom we remember from *Prinsloo of Prinsloosdorp*. He co-opts Sarel and his commando into ambushing a British convoy sent to relieve Ladysmith with provisions. Sarel's stake in this misadventure is to be one thousand pounds, and the ambush at Bokmans Drift is the central episode of the novel. Sarel is scrupulous about not giving the command to attack himself, deferring to Brink, who conducts the entire operation. It is a model of a peaceful engagement, as no one beyond a few black drivers gets hurt, and only a few of the thousand head of cattle are injured. Sarel is so unwilling to inflict damage on anyone at all that he even hands over the cleaning up of the scene of chaos and confusion—as drivers, wagons, provisions, and newcomer British recruits pile up in a steep ravine—to their British officer. At Bokmans Drift, whisky flows once again, an impromptu party is thrown, and both British and Boer soldiers feast on the greatest display of food and drink that either side has seen for many a day. Brink slips off with the cattle, which he resells to the British at another point down the line, and Sarel in a sense is vindicated by having supplied his men with loot at the same time as avoiding dealing the British a mortal blow. In a curious way, honor is satisfied on both sides.

The same is true of the next episode in which Sarel tangles with Brink's stepdaughter, the attractive Charlotte, a girl working for her father in the business of duping both sides, and a superb manipulator of doting men. At General Joubert's express will, Sarel is instructed to accompany Charlotte on a mission to effect an arranged escape of a British officer and expert in heliographic code from the Model School in Pretoria (where, incidentally, Winston Churchill was also held prisoner of war). Charlotte induces Sarel to fall hopelessly in love with her, for she is everything that Sarel is learning to adore most in British colonial culture—she is lithe, witty, socially gracious, and highly educated, having been to a finishing school.

This incongruous pair, the wily flirt and the genial backwoodsman, take wartime Pretoria by storm, Charlotte leading Sarel by the nose. Sarel is bankrupt by the end of the venture, having bought her every item of haberdashery in town. Together they burgle an uncle of hers to the tune of three thousand pounds. With the escaped British captain in tow, Katrina the intended discovers them and gives chase, intent on claiming her future husband and her capital. The trio just manage to return to the lines. There Sarel and the Boers are double-crossed, as the captain has no intention of turning coat and joining the Boers as a spy—rather, he escapes with the doting Charlotte to Natal, leaving Sarel a disillusioned man. He is, naturally, also left culpable for the stolen money, which remnants of his own commando steal from him in turn. What is more, Sarel's heart is broken and, having had enough of the vagaries of fortune and love, he is ready for a final capitulation.

Throughout his maneuvers at the front his constant companion has been an old-style Boer, Paul du Plooy, a character who is virtually a living legend in South African fiction. He is the "last of the Takhaars," so named after his uncut and unkempt, branchlike hair. Oom Paul (Uncle Paul, a surrogate Kruger figure) is a bitter-ender, a Pentateuch-spouting Dopper, or Baptist, whose motto is never to say die in the face of overwhelming odds. Old Paul, a septuagenarian, haunts Sarel like an incubus. Their relationship is by turns profoundly irritating, touching, and rewarding to Sarel. Paul frequently revives his flagging spirits and, when all is lost, the two of them form the last flanking movement of the campaign. Their vengeance is directed neither against the Boers nor the Rooineks, but against the profiteers like Brink who have been the only winners in the war situation. This two-man justice squad has different motives, however, as each things Brink should be exposed and delivered up to a different side.

The penultimate episode in the novel involves this rounding up of Brink, who takes both Sarel and Paul prisoner and, his own double game having become somewhat perilous, decides to try and leave Natal and make for Delagoa Bay. Here, however, rapid reversals are the order of the day. Sarel is induced to join Brink and Paul is left behind (his hair jammed in a chest of drawers), but Paul escapes and rounds them both up. On a deserted plain, a huge patch of scorched earth left behind by the armies, Paul and Brink fight out the real battle of the work, the battle between old-time values backed up by superb marksmanship and the new-time values of trickery and deceit. Brink eventually buys even Oom Paul off. Without admitting their defeat, Sarel and Paul settle for a deposit slip, which they think is a cheque or banking credit note. The true villain, Brink—who, it turns out, was an Englishman all along—finally escapes, and Sarel can no longer return to General Joubert with a credible story and a captive to show for it. So he and Paul devise a scheme whereby Sarel will at last escape both his debts and his Katrina, which is this: Paul leaves for the Boer lines with a perfectly formulated story, chapter and verse included, about how Sarel bravely has died in defense of his country, as indeed many a patriotic commando fighter died in the name of the ailing, outwitted Z.A.R.

For Sarel, then, all that is left to him is to settle his debts with the British, whom we know he has secretly, if somewhat ambiguously, supported throughout. He limps into Pietermaritzburg and surrenders, hoping that he will be accepted as a prisoner and let out for the rest of the war on parole. By a last stroke of bad fortune, a newspaper interviewer reports that he had been resident in Natal before the war and even applied for voting rights in British territory; thus, Sarel is given the status of rebel, and the second trial of the work ensues. This trial is as unfair as the first one, and we know now the full story of the agony of a man caught in a polarized situation. Sarel's innately gentle approach to mankind is here twisted round into resembling a blood-thirstiness and a malice which we know to be beyond him.

Charlotte resurfaces guiltily to repair some of the damage she has caused in Sarel's life, by paying his defense fees. But not one detail of the true complexity of Sarel's tale appears at the trial. He is sentenced merely for being a Boer to a year's imprisonment and a fine of two hundred and fifty pounds. This, together with his being shown the engagement ring Charlotte has from the British officer he helped escape, causes his profound dejection: "This broke my heart, and hope died,"[12] he comments simply.

The novel ends with Sarel still in prison, with a few weeks to run on his sentence. He knows that Charlotte has escaped to England with her captain, and that Katrina, thinking him dead, has married a cousin. When the prison doors open, he will face a ruined Transvaal, defeated and hopeless like himself, and for his pains be even deeper in debt than ever, his cattle gone. His name, however, will have lived on as a legend in the Boer world as the embodiment of the noble and brave fighter who never deserted the cause of freedom. But the cause, we know, has broken him. Sarel will have to reconstruct his life under British control; he is doomed to face a future for which he is barely qualified, with the load of the past weighing heavily on his shoulders. Thus, Blackburn's saga of the Burgher Don Quixote, a man whose confused but humane ideals are shattered in a relentlessly material world, whose quest for honor, decency, and justice was doomed even before it got underway.

Put in those terms, the issues in Blackburn's *A Burgher Quixote* seem clear enough. But Sarel the buffoon is unaware of most of the factors that steer the course of his life, and so the reader is placed in a position of having to gather almost the entire story by implication. The ironic gap between what the first-person narrator sees and what the reader sees has never been wider in Blackburn. Truly, *A Burgher Quixote* is one of Blackburn's most devious, ingenious, and refreshing works, revealing an adroitness, a technique and style that are unequalled in all of his work. The comparison with Cervantes's *Don Quixote* that Blackburn invites in this novel is not to be taken lightly. The hero with an Old-World code of honor placed unwillingly in a modern world supposedly without honor is common to both of them. The ironic gap is not only between points of view, but between ways of being and, like Cervantes before him, Blackburn exposes the defects of the former system in the light of the barbarities of its successor. And like Cervantes's novel, Blackburn's has an elegiac tone which mourns the state of the world and lost chivalries.

In *A Burgher Quixote,* however, Blackburn's technique is quite different from Cervantes's. Blackburn does not write in his own voice, as Cervantes does, but assumes the mask of his dummy figure, Sarel. Like *Prinsloo of Prinsloosdorp* and like *Kruger's Secret Service, A*

The Sarel Erasmus Satires

Burgher Quixote purports to be a real document by a living man (although, this time, signed by Blackburn). We are never unaware, throughout the progress of the narrative, of the situation in which it is supposedly written: it is a jail account, penned by Sarel in direst circumstances. Indeed, he himself invites comparison with other writers trapped in prison, notably Sir Walter Raleigh and John Bunyan. (Cervantes himself would have been an appropriate addition.) Although we do not know until the very end on which side of the line Sarel is languishing, or why, we are never unaware that this document is a cry from a man in distress, a man trying to make sense of the turmoil of his existence after the event. Thus, movingly and circuitously, the whole of *A Burgher Quixote* is an apologia and a justification addressed to his judges and conquerors.

In the last analysis, it is also a record of all the thousand and one human details that were taken into the war zone and never reported on by the war correspondents. This is the novel of individual human experience that newspaper reporting flattens and denies, come from the depths of a soul struggling to master the pain, confusion, and split identity that Blackburn saw the war bringing to the land. It also happens to be the only novel of stature to have emerged from the South African War—the last of the gentlemen's wars, but the first of the twentieth-century wars as well.

Such was also the opinion of much of the press that reviewed *A Burgher Quixote*. In the editorial column of *Blackwood's Magazine*, after describing the factual background of the novel, the advance reviewer states:

> it is a model of irony, simple and sustained. Nowhere is there any faltering, nor any forgetfulness of the method employed. And how great this achievement is will be understood if we consider the few ironists that our literature may boast. To the ironist one temptation is constant: he becomes so earnest in his desire to prove his point that he drops into argument, or even into morality. Of this cardinal sin Sarel Erasmus is always guiltless. He never knows, what is patent to the reader, that he is a sorry scamp. He preserves from beginning to end the beautiful appearance of simplicity, which makes the most dastardly of his actions seem respectable. It is true that Mr Blackburn had already shown how great is his power of satire. But his *Burgher Quixote* will manifestly increase his reputation, and we recommend this masterpiece of irony to our readers, not merely because it will teach them a profound lesson of South Africa . . . but because it is packed with amusement, and prompts a smile with every page.[13]

An even more fulsome review of *A Burgher Quixote*, subsequently used as an advertisement for the book throughout South Africa, was the following from *The Natal Witness:* "The author of *Prinsloo of Prinsloosdorp* has given us another work, which will be read with entertainment by all who appreciate the best of fiction with a firm basis in fact. Among the scores of novels written in the late war the *Burgher Quixote* will stand out foremost in its power of literary expression and striking humorous portraiture."[14]

So, *A Burgher Quixote* was not only enthusiastically received but seemed at the time to stand out head and shoulders above the proliferation of other works the war produced. Notable among these, for our purposes, was *My Reminiscences of the Anglo-Boer War* by Commandant Ben Viljoen, Blackburn's successor on the *Transvaal Sentinel* and Sarel's nemesis; many of the episodes in *A Burgher Quixote,* particularly the "Bokmans Drift" raid, appear in their real versions in Viljoen's memoir, and the friendship between Viljoen and Blackburn must rank as one of the most productive in terms of South African literary history. The war was refought in an unprecedented number of books, pamphlets, memoirs, autobiographies, and so on, because, for England, it was not only the biggest of the hundred or so colonial wars fought in the nineteenth century, but it was, in terms of newsmaking events, the one closest to home. Interest in the Boer, of course, could not have been higher than in 1903, now that the British Empire had subdued him and added him to the fold of nations under its sway.

It is to this new circumstance that Sarel Erasmus addresses himself. In *A Burgher Quixote* his intended readership is the British people. He is being tried in their eyes, and to them he makes his appeal. For this reason he elects to write in English, a rather self-conscious English, to be sure, but one which Blackburn uses faultlessly. For an audience proficient in the literary English of Edwardian days, encountering the word order, syntax, and idiom of the Taal transposed into English must have been a striking experience. Blackburn is skillful at pulling the most incongruous turns of phrase around into pathos, often letting Sarel's English crumble and flounder when he is being most personal. At points where he is under stress in his narrative, language fails him, as it were; his mastery of the language correlates with his emotional well-being.

Yet even the most urbane passages are flecked with misuses and abuses of English—"sun-up" for sunrise (*BQ,* 138); "it was needful that . . ." (*BQ*, 132). Blackburn uses such awkward phraseology not to indicate how lacking in proficiency Sarel is—the contrary is clearly the case—but subtly to remind us that we are being addressed by a non-English-speaker who is using our own language in an attempt to touch us in the terms which we understand best. Sarel's struggle to learn the language is also, obviously, a proof of his sympathy for, and fascination with, things English. His language alone validates his claim that he is a man trying to grow out of his lost, constricted backwater world into a community which stretched around the known world and on which, as the slogan was, the sun never set. (Likewise, Ben Viljoen in real life took to writing a novel explaining the Boer way of life in English and had it successfully published in Boston once he had become an American citizen.)[15]

Sarel's English is heavily derived from his reading of books. A somewhat awkward literariness marks his editorializing. This is used by Blackburn as character-building, and the following paragraphs, which serve as a bridge in the action, are a fair example:

I have noticed, among other great peculiarities of the English that make them so different to us Afrikanders, one thing very particularly, and that not only in their talk, but in their books and newspaper writings. It is their obstinate refusal to confess like men that they know fear. How often have I heard young Rooineks, fresh come to the country, boasting of being in danger, such as in crossing a river in flood, or going close to a smallpox ambulance, and even playing cards during a thunderstorm, and saying they were not frightened. Now all this is vain boasting and unseemly, for it is natural and religious for men to have fear, as the Bible often shows; and for a man to proclaim that he knows not the godly feeling, which is given us that we may keep out of danger, is to confess himself a blasphemer. We Afrikanders are much more honest in this thing, for we are not ashamed to declare openly when we are afraid; and there is no phrase more often on our lips than, "I got a bad schrick," which means, "I had a bad fright," a thing no Rooinek would say, his vanity and ignorance of the Bible preventing him from being truthful in such matters. We have seen how dangerous such foolishness may be in war-time, for again and again, if the British had been more fearful, they would not have had so many of their soldiers killed.

As one who knows what danger is, through having heard my parents and old voortrekkers tell of the terrible calamities that befell them in the veld from Kafirs, lightning, and wild beasts, I am not ashamed to say that I freely own when I feel fear, not having become arrogant and boastful through my close contact with Rooineks. (*BQ*, 290–91)

This passage says, on the surface, that Sarel frankly admits to the power of fear over a man—indeed, the work is replete with examples of Boers so terrified of the Khaki's lyddite and bayonets that they turn tail at the thought of them. But Sarel sees unreasonable bravery as a kind of folly, even stupidity. Yet the action of the book shows that Sarel is extremely courageous in little things, unthinkingly and unself-consciously, and utterly fearless when it comes to matters affecting his own vanity and prowess. The other side of this coin is that he finds the obedient, efficient, loyal, disciplined type of soldier—the enemy captain is the outstanding example—unnatural. He pretends to admire such a one, but in truth is filled with loathing for such mechanical perfection. The two sides of the battleline exemplify this: the Boer commandoes shamble forth using their common sense and their initiative; the British move in ranks behind their hardware, obedient to the last man, unable to adapt to the terrain except by obliterating it. Fear—the great taboo element in men's hearts during warfare—is hardly talked about in other war fiction, and fear is the subject upon which Sarel, the world's greatest liar, is most honest.

Sarel's honesty about warfare is collocated with his honesty about love. At the point in the novel when Sarel is most tricked by circumstances, where Charlotte makes off with her captain, deserting Sarel, the morals of the captain come through to us in his letter written in apology to Sarel: "All's fair in love and war." All is, in fact, pretty unfair in both, the love affair being the one that defeats Sarel more severely than any battle. Seldom in South African fiction has a love affair been so tenderly and carefully dramatized. Almost the entire course of the development of Sarel's love for Charlotte is unstated. Possibly he himself is not fully aware of the depths to which it shakes him, but the work gains eloquence, paradoxically, from his inability to express himself fully at any of the crucial points. What makes the affair most poignant, for us, is that the smallest details—Charlotte brushing his hand, Charlotte asking for a new dress—are recorded with a complete clarity, while Sarel refrains from uttering any of his wildest hopes or fears about what such details might mean. The work fairly explodes with a bursting of hopeful, fearful love as a result; Sarel's reticence is something we feel as the most intense self-control. For him we can only have a hugely generous sympathy.

The Sarel Erasmus Satires

What makes the love theme sharply defined is that, like the war theme, it is always framed in a context of clumsy farce. In fact, the entire power of *A Burgher Quixote*, in the end, lies in the blending of the idiotic with the tragic. On the one hand is Katrina, the two-hundred-pound hoyden who, when she finds Sarel in a railway carriage with Charlotte, grabs him by the hair and knocks him senseless. On the other is Charlotte, who at her most gracious and delectable, is manipulating him as shamefully. In Katrina's path Sarel gives way to abject terror and, at a point where Katrina's sponge of a brother intrudes on Sarel's key lovemaking scene with Charlotte, Sarel even resorts to violence, hitting him with a bottle. (This, after the putative brother-in-law has wasted ages in his drunkenness by insisting on going down stairs backward to maintain his dignity.)

Funnier and more aggravating still is the feedback Sarel gets from old Paul, his only confessor in the novel, on matters amatorial:

> . . . Paul was quite unable to understand my great grief at finding my affection for Charlotte sown on barren soil. Love, in its noble and inspiring form, as practised in England and in stories and plays, has no meaning for a Boer, who looks upon it as foolishness; and Paul could know nothing of it, for he was first married at sixteen years of age, and, as he lost each wife, took others quickly, not having even the trouble of seeking them; for he was always well off with cattle, had two good farms, and stood well in the kerk. . . . So high did he stand as a marrying man, that all through his district he was looked upon as a safe stand-by; for, somehow, it was felt that he would frequently fall into widowerhood, as he did, and his next wife was fixed upon by the vrouws, who were always correct in their guessing. Thus it came that, women being much after him, he held them in light esteem; and there is a story that he once put one of his wives to help the Kafirs draw the plough as a punishment. (*BQ*, 278–79)

The reader may blench at the implications of the rough humor of a passage like the above, but it comes from a world where exigencies of the life force and the urge to tame the land are one, and the chauvinist autocrat and patriarch rides supreme.

In contradistinction to this is the world of "stories and plays," the world of romantic love, which to Sarel is synonymous with education and civilization. The same conflict between the two ways of life is the essence of Schreiner's *The Story of an African Farm*, which Blackburn knew and admired. Like Lyndall or Waldo in

Schreiner's work, Sarel is also thwarted in his attempts to escape the rural world in favor of the delicate and cultivated social world of the English novel and drama. In the gallery of romantic heroes, Sarel Erasmus is truly a clod and an uncouth fellow, but that is not to say that he, too, does not experience the finest shades of feeling open to a man. Indeed, trying to express "finer feelings" becomes an obsession with him, and he learns all too painfully that "sarcasm" and "irony" are the ways of hiding hurt feelings in the more refined modes of expression.

There is internal evidence in the novel that in writing *A Burgher Quixote* Blackburn had more than the novels and plays of his day as a model for Sarel. Just as he was reviving the strategies of a writer like Cervantes, so was he reverting to an older form of satire which seemed well and truly lost within British literary tradition. The key to this is, in fact, in Sarel's own surname, Erasmus. About this, Sarel has the following to say:

It appears even now passing strange to my mind that an Erasmus should have to explain to the world who he is before beginning to tell of his doings. Time was, and that not many years ago, when my father and I, riding up to a farm in any district, would have no need to tell our names; but so vast has now become the inhabitants of this country, that a man may be excused for not quickly realising to which branch of the Erasmus family a Sarel belongs; and I fear this ignorance will increase now that so many strangers have come into the land who do not even know the name, and much less recognise the great likeness we Erasmuses all bear to our common ancestor. This was the case when I arrived at Maritzburg as a prisoner of war.
"What name did you say?" asked the British officer who received me.
"Sarel Erasmus."
"How do you spell it?" was the surprising answer.
"Sir," replied I with great dignity, "I am a descendant of that Erasmus who translated the first Greek Testament and taught you English true religion."
"Sorry I have not the pleasure of the gentleman's acquaintance," said he, haughtily, the foolish fellow being plainly ignorant that that Erasmus lived nearly five hundred years ago; and I had to pronounce the name several times, and even write it before he could recognise it. (*BQ*, 2–3)

While Sarel proudly claims descent from the leader of the European Reformation, Erasmus of Rotterdam, the humanist and Protestant, Blackburn claims descent from the other side of the Erasmus family tradition. Erasmus of Rotterdam also wrote *The Praise of Folly* in 1511, a homiletic satire which, while pretending to praise hypocrisy, self-delusion, boasting, and narrow-mindedness, in fact used deadpan satire to let the light of reason shine into the dark pretences of the European mind. *A Burgher Quixote* performs much the same function, or at least that is the intention of the tactics deployed in the Erasmus manner.

The targets are predictable Blackburn favorites—the capitalist face of colonial expansionism and the injustice of justice. But these Blackburn themes seem to be put into a new context in *A Burgher Quixote,* as though the war itself had temporarily swept what he saw as the main issues of the day to one side. (Blackburn would return to them with a vengeance in his next novel, *Leaven.*) But in *A Burgher Quixote,* the main issue, which is related to capitalist expansionism, seems to be class consciousness, a social idea imported from Britain and which is utterly alien to a man like Sarel. Class consciousness, however, is the real cause of his undoing.

As Blackburn wrote on this subject to *Chambers's Journal* in 1902, as he was completing *A Burgher Quixote:*

Most Britons on arriving in South Africa are struck by the utter absence of the class distinctions he has known at home; and the Colonial in turn finds it almost impossible to grasp the ideas of "class" and social strata. He cannot understand how a man who has resided in an English town is not personally acquainted with the most exalted inhabitants thereof; and many a new-comer has been under suspicion as an impostor or as having a past to conceal because he has had to confess to never having met certain distinguished fellow-countrymen. Every Colonial is personally acquainted with his public representatives, from the Governor and Prime-Minister downwards, and he cannot conceive how an Englishman could live in London without being on friendly terms with Lord Salisbury or the Colonial Secretary. The Colonial is essentially a democrat—until he makes money and visits England. Class distinctions are utterly beyond him. . . .[16]

Blackburn makes one large exception to this—the rigid distinction drawn between the white and "nonwhite"—but within the white members of the cast of *A Burgher Quixote* those who are either Boers or Colonial-born English-speakers are free of a sense of class distinctions.

Sarel's career is evidence of this all the way. Not only does he stroll into the tent of the commanding officer, General Piet Joubert, without even announcing himself, but he feels quite free to amble up the pathway of President Kruger's house to chat with him on the veranda. (In the event he does not do this in this novel, but certainly not for reasons of class distinction or protocol.) Nor are there class distinctions within his own ragged commando. The squad members elect their own functionaries, like the quartermaster, the keeper of the horses, and the scouts, and every action is individually fought on a voluntary basis. Exclusivity does work within this small society, but it is on the basis of religion, not class. On Sundays when old Paul gives vent to his interminable preaching in the most droning High Dutch, not only true sons of the soil attend his services, but Irish Catholics, Polish Jews, and English heathen (with heathen blacks on the fringes). Much good-humored fun is occasioned by the way church services that go on too long are interrupted by drinking bouts featuring English music-hall love songs and ballads, the godless words of which many of the Burghers do not understand. True-blooded Burghers are as attracted to the gambling tables and booze as the paroled criminals and ruffians among them who set them up.

This democratic classlessness among whites is carefully demonstrated throughout the novel, particularly in respect of uniforms: the Burgher forces have no prescribed uniforms, and each man wears what he can scrounge and fancies is appropriate to the occasion. One of the delectable byplays here is that Blackburn has Sarel choose himself a uniform which is some sort of fantasy garment ordered from a Jewish shopkeeper for a sanitary inspector. The Burghers may all appear similar, as Sarel remarks, because they have no razors and grow beards, but within this uniformity there is no ranking or status acquisition. Indeed, the Burghers come and go so freely from their homes that there is also no line to be drawn between combatant and civilian population. Nor are military commands given; old men lead through giving "advice" (*BQ,* 137). The Burghers are also united in poverty, for their war service is unpaid and due to the inefficiencies of the commissariat they are often close to starvation.

Given this one reservation about the color line, it was this fluid society without a class hierarchy that Blackburn so admired. Rotten with corruption though it may have been, the Z.A.R. was to him a fine example of a socialist society in principle and in action. What is more, each of Blackburn's Transvaal backvelders combines the extremes of the class spectrum within one man—Sarel Erasmus is

The Sarel Erasmus Satires 93

a natural aristocrat, who has middle-class aspirations, and yet is a working man. As Sarel remarks, he is also related to just about everyone in the Transvaal in an immense network of clandom and kinship. All Sarel's petty violations of the law must be seen in this light. As a public prosecutor he had much experience of springing the members of his vastly extended family, while fighting intrusion by twisting the law to condemn any outsider. At the outset the very family bond calls him back to the Transvaal to defend a relative, and lands him unwillingly back within the race apart.

The role of blacks, meanwhile, within this utopian society is an ignominious and intolerable one, though Sarel is so unable to see this that he hardly mentions them within the course of his complaint. Yet Blackburn affords us the spectacle of their dispossession and humiliation in persistently subtle details. Frequently Sarel has his only horse saddled up and is off, only to arrive at his destination with the same "Kafir" in his company; we realize that this "Kafir" must have run the entire route. Blacks loyal to the Natal farmers once imprison Sarel and old Paul, but are so afraid of Boer vengeance that they let our heroes go. Andries Brink's "schelm Kafirs" manage a massive spy network, carrying messages to and fro and reporting to him on all military operations with impunity. Sarel never sees that this is so, and makes the fatal mistake of not crediting them with the intelligence to conduct intelligence work. The black-white class distinction is not, however, an issue to Sarel, who assumes the peasantry will remain subservient more or less for ever. Blackburn leaves the matter there in *A Burgher Quixote,* which remains a paean to the everyday socialism of the Boers in the field, the willing, naive, homely Boers who could not compete against the arrival of the technologically superior British. In time, the British would break them by segregating them sexually—men in prisoner of war camps overseas, women and children in relocation centers in towns— and into many gradations of class after the war.

Sarel, naturally, remains relatively unenlightened on these issues; they are beyond his comprehension, and the satire works better that way. But as in *Richard Hartley, Prospector,* Blackburn does bring a spokesman for his views into the picture in a brief interlude passage before the end, when the leading characters are marooned in the Drakensberg mountains. Once more, we as readers seem to be brought to Blackburn's Loteni retreat for a moral exchange with our hermit sage. This time the sage figure is a prospector; to all intents and purposes, he might as well be Richard Hartley himself. His name, however, is Mark Capper, a solitary man surviving beyond the reach of a world from which he has defected. He has hardly heard of the war that rages around him, yet he does have a reason for having turned his back on the haunts of men: he prefers the company of animals, and his Eden is replete with weird pets—a puff-adder, an iguana, a crow with a broken leg, a tiger-cat, and a striped mouse which he keeps in a basin at night.

Capper's integrity and probing questions bring Brink the villain to the edge of self-realization, and Sarel listens to Brink with the sting of understanding:

"I was reckoning up only to-day, Mark, having a little time for quiet thought. First there was illicit diamond buying at Kimberley,—the shortcut to wealth and respectability or the breakwater; contractor to the troops in three native wars,—profitable, but requiring too much handiness at cooking accounts; slave-dealer, otherwise native labor agent,—profitable, but dirty, and opposed to my early religious education. Then illicit liquor-dealer on the Rand,—most profitable, but dirtiest business of all; and, grandest of all, purveyor of arms to the native races. I was reckoning up to-day, Mark, that more than half the rifles owned by natives in the Transvaal and Natal have been supplied by me at an average of a tenner apiece. That means a lot of trouble coming for the whites presently. . . . Few Boers ever met me without being worse for it in property and morals, for I helped to sow the seeds of race hatred that has brought about the war, and will end in the absorption of Boerdom. That is where my patriotic British sentiment is fed up. What I don't like is the knowledge that I have helped spoil a promising race." (*BQ*, 323–24)

These views might well have been Blackburn's own; the fear of Native uprisings would occupy him in *Leaven* and *Love Muti,* and the catalog of criminal British incursions on Boerdom is the subject of *Secret Service in South Africa.* The spoiled promise, however, is the central subject of his most mournful and persuasive work, the *Burgher Quixote* we have in hand.

Although *A Burgher Quixote* is one of Blackburn's lengthiest novels (only *Richard Hartley, Prospector* and *Love Muti* approach it in length), the final impression the reader has of the novel is one of sparseness, of stringent economy. The tempo is never slowed by evocative descriptions or wordy meditations; rather, it is devoid of almost all local coloring. So tightly written is it that old Paul's long hair is first mentioned only when it is the means of his entrapment, and Sarel does not describe himself until page 329. So thoroughly does Sarel write from within the situation that he allows almost no concessions to a reader who might not obviously understand each moment.

Blackburn wishes to illustrate Sarel's parochialism, to be sure, but this also means that the novel is not cluttered with explanatory passages (like *Richard Hartley, Prospector*). All description in the work functions relatively, in a process of cross-referencing. For instance, when Sarel is taken under guard to the British commander in Pietermaritzburg, expecting a red carpet and a welcome, he merely comments: "We were taken to the commandant, who sat at a desk in an office just as if he had been a clerk at Pretoria" (*BQ*, 327). This understatement not only gives us a sense of Sarel's disappointment, but, quite incidentally, fills us in on what Pretoria must have been like a hundred pages earlier.

The same sparseness is used in emotional descriptions: "the dust fell from my eyes and the hardness went out of my heart" (*BQ*, 92–93). More like Sancho Panza than Don Quixote, Sarel is given to encapsulating situations in aphorisms and epigrams, always of a folk origin: "when the glitter of gold is in the eye of a Boer he can see no more than an owl in the sunshine" (*BQ*, 158). "Love," Sarel comments, for him "is above oxen" (*BQ*, 274). "Stop this Bible language," Sarels tells old Paul, "and tell me in the plain Taal where are the Burghers!" (*BQ*, 265). Despite his supposed impatience with biblical rhetoric and his distrust of big words—he specifically hectors the reader on this point—some of Blackburn's most moving insights are achieved through biblical cadence: "And many of the Burghers saw it as Paul wished them to, and his fame as an interpreter of the Bible was increased" (*BQ*, 61). Much of Sarel's experience of life and of language is drawn from the rural, cattle-keeping world of the prophetic books of the Old Testament that fitted so appositely the Boer way of life. We also realize how extremely intimately Blackburn knew that world and its language.

Sarel's own style contrasts brutally with the style of the Natal press that makes an exhibit of him and, incidentally, gives us our first actual view of what Sarel looked like. The report is headed "The Latest Capture" and reads as follows:

The monotony of khaki that pervades the city was agreeably broken yesterday. Parading Church Street, at a deliberate pace that gave full opportunity for inspection and admiration, was a young man arrayed in a uniform whose identification puzzled the authorities on service sartorials. Imagine a blue mess-jacket, intended for a warrior forty-five round the chest, enveloping in its flabby folds a thirty-four inch measurement, the numerous green braid frogs and facings suggesting the ornaments of a lady's zouave jacket. Sleeves bedizened with the broad gold stripes of a sergeant, cuffs of a mailboat steward, and green collar and bright gilt buttons the size of half-crowns, trousers a shade of brighter blue than the jacket, very narrow, but broadly striped with green. A small, sharp-featured, close-eyed face with incipient moustache and shaggy black beard, half concealed by a wide-spreading smasher hat. This gaudy and original get-up covered the five-foot-six personality of Commandant Sarel Erasmus, late Public Prosecutor of Prinsloosdorp, and, later, Chief of General Joubert's flying column of Taakhaars and Reimschoons. . . . (BQ, 329)

So much for our twenty-eight-year-old hero, the jaunty buffoon with a feather in his cap. While he is in prison, President Kruger goes into exile and Queen Victoria dies. An age of spirited individuality dies as well.

And so, in a way, dies the whole world of the picaresque adventure hero, at least in South Africa. With the battle for supremacy fought out between Britain and the Boer, a period of reconstruction on the British model is ahead. Standardization and conformity crimp the rule of fortune and chance, the standby of the opportunist on the loose, freewheeling through experiences of a bewildering complexity with the guiding hand of Providence as an incentive and a challenge. Gone also is the world of the Quixotic spirit, the spirit of the loser who tried only to humanize the bedevilments of an encroaching destiny, and who mistook windmills for giants.

I Came and Saw

But in 1908 Blackburn was to pull another trick with the satirical picaresque formula, with Sarel Erasmus, once more, as his hero in a world gone awry—the postwar world of Edwardian society. So comfortable was Blackburn with his Burgher mouthpiece that he obviously felt he could accompany him on one last splendid adventure.

I Came and Saw is the third volume of the trilogy. The title is derived from Julius Caesar's famous boast about Britain, *Veni, vidi, vici*—I came, I saw, I conquered. In Sarel's case, the coming and seeing is in evidence, but the conquering is hardly appropriate. Sarel is now a British subject of the Transvaal, and his visit to "Home" in *I Came and Saw* is merely an extension of his defeat.

The essence of the satire in *I Came and Saw* is a timely turning of the tables on Blackburn's part. Previously, all his fiction had dealt with either the local inhabitants in an overseas society, or with the case of the colonizer sent out to deal with colonial problems and finding a home in those far-flung outposts. This time, with devastating effect, Blackburn reversed the norms of colonial fiction to send a colonial to the metropolis, a colonial whom we know thoroughly well and to whom what the European reader takes for granted is strange and unknown. The result of this reversal is a delightful innovation in the fiction of South Africa. *I Came and Saw* is the first novel in the category of the "Colonial's Revenge."

In his forewords to *I Came and Saw,* Sarel Erasmus explains his motivation:

> having now agreed to work hand-in-hand with the Englander in the Transvaal, it is but right that we should know all that is possible about those we are so implicitly trusting, though so far away from our observation. . . . Being so much better educated than the average Boer, I am the better fitted to spy out the land, either in its fullness or its nakedness, while my habit as a one-time public prosecutor of believing no one, however honest, and always suspecting lies at the bottom of statements, even before the witness has sworn to speak the truth, makes it hard for me to be deceived.[17]

He is indeed an ideal "spy" for Blackburn's purposes, being canny, suspicious of motives, and an inveterate seeker after his own truths. As usual, it is not Sarel who arrives at much of the truth, the whole truth, and nothing but the truth, during his elaborate peregrinations in *I Came and Saw,* but the reader.

To the reader Blackburn addresses these words in his author's note, as if he wishes to make sure how *I Came and Saw* should be read:

> The author is conscious that many readers may have some difficulty in reconciling the almost childish simplicity of Sarel Erasmus with his claim to the dignity of a Public Prosecutor and Law Agent. . . . As is usually the case everywhere with the lonely country-reared youth whose education and knowledge of the world have been acquired by an undirected and ill-

assimilated general reading, this type of "educated" young Boer is amusingly superficial and priggish. He speaks and writes "proper" English in an inflated quasi-academical style, often the misused legacy of one of the itinerant Scottish sailors who, as farm tutors, used to be the principal instructors of young Boerdom. (*ICS*, vii–viii)

Sarel's style in *I Came and Saw* may still be somewhat lofty and formal, but the gap between his learned English and the situations to which it is put to describe is the major stylistic achievement of the novel. As ever with Blackburn, his tongue is firmly in his cheek, and nothing is quite what it appears to be. Sarel's "childish simplicity" is seldom in evidence, and then only when he is duped, and then that quality is hardly seen to be deplorable, looked down upon, or denigrated. Sarel may also be "destitute of the most elementary educational qualifications," but the novel itself is full of examples of British destitutes. While Sarel holds them in awesome wonder, Blackburn shows how our self-made man shines besides the Yahoos of the educated establishment. Sarel may also be "amusingly superficial and priggish," but the novel brings to the fore a gallery of such superficiality and priggishness unprecedented in Blackburn. Sarel is not the one at whom the satire is primarily directed.

Under the terms of the Peace of Vereeniging that concluded the South African War in 1902, the late Transvaal Republic was to be awarded a degree of autonomy under the governor-generalship of the states of South Africa. The plot of *I Came and Saw* opens with Sarel Erasmus a defeated candidate in an election for the Transvaal Legislative Assembly. Sarel's defeat is widely reported in the "reptile Uitlander press," which remains a constant aggravation in all of Blackburn's satires, and "as an indication of the good feeling now existing between the two races" (*ICS*, xxii) Sarel is at a loose end without income; in fact, his campaign debts drive him to devise a scheme whereby he can evade his creditors. A new factor in the Sarel story is that he is now finally married, to Katrina (not the same one), a dour woman who spends much of her time visiting her relatives in Pretoria and thirsting after the latest gossip and fashions in clothing from overseas. To evade her as well, Sarel sneaks out of the Transvaal once more to find his fortune.

This time he is in the company of a Rand millionaire, the type of Cockney the music halls sang about, dripping with vulgar wealth.

He is Mr. Robert Magnus, who has risen to fortune through all the predictable Blackburn channels: illicit liquor dealing, buying and selling of scrip, and financing of oversubscribed gold mines. In terms of history, Blackburn is once again scrupulously accurate. The gold industry was in a postwar decline, its labor force scattered by the disorder of the occupation of the Witwatersrand, and we are in the brief period when in mid-decade the employers of mineworkers resorted to importing Chinese labor onto the mines. Bob Magnus is moved to return to England to raise British capital for a new mining venture, which is to reestablish the employment of South African blacks at lower wages than the semiskilled Chinese, and to restore confidence in South African mining in general. Sarel has a hold on Bob, knowing all the shady workings of his rise from rags to riches, and has himself received kickbacks from Bob for turning a blind eye to his chain of canteens across the Rand.

Thus, the two operators set off, working hand in glove—Bob the confidence man and Sarel his private secretary, keeper of the purse. They are a model team for the new British South Africa. They are also a team with many historical precedents, for a previous novelist—F. R. Statham—had satirized the late Cecil Rhodes under the name of Magnus before.[18] No South African tycoon had ever had such a strange secretary in tow, however, and one of the most affecting strengths of Blackburn's account is the mutual shyness and interdependence which develops between the two throughout their operation.

In Cape Town before embarking on that favorite institution of the imperial heyday, a Union-Castle ocean liner, Sarel feels it fitting to prepare himself educationally by reading all the literature on Great Britain in the Young Men's Christian Association. The morally uplifting pamphlets he comes across become one of the central targets of the work:

Among the things that I read was a story of a missionary who took to England with him a Kaffir, and gained much credit from the people who foolishly and readily believed all the stupid stories told about this boy being a Brand snatched from the Burning, an Example of Regeneration and a Symbol of the Destruction of the Old Adam in the Dark Continent. Though I was not quite clear as to the meaning of these phrases, the idea struck me as excellent. (*ICS*, 16)

The third member of the invading team thus becomes Sixpence, alias Makalagalibie, whom Sarel describes as follows: "having just come out of jail and being known to the police, [he] was not eager to stay in town. He was a Pondo, I think, a mongrel race, half town, half kraal, and largely in jail. He spoke English and Dutch. I should have preferred a Zulu, as they are cleaner and finer looking, and, not being Christian, have very few vices" (*ICS*, 19). With his convert in tow, Sarel boards the ship to enter a world which is both larger, rounder, and more far-reaching in roguery than even he had suspected.

With his face "like the ten commandments" (*ICS*, 18) and with his wide smasher hat and trim beard, Sarel has the devil's own job trying to persuade those he encounters on board ship that as a Boer he is neither black nor shaggy all over. As he frequently reminds us again, he is a descendant of the very Erasmus who brought civilization to England. This time, however, he is mercilessly ragged by the British passengers and crew: "no Englander can pronounce my name properly, with a broad sounding 'A,' as it should be, being not Sarel, rhyming with carol, but broad Sahrel Erahsmus" (*ICS*, 26).

Sarel's first impressions of England are ingenuously recorded:

I am not so ignorant as not to perceive that in many things England is a good land, but it has many drawbacks, and I cannot but think that the land is better than its people, who do not deserve such a good country— except their horrible climate, which is so bad that the first thing an Englander remarks when he meets another is, "It's a fine day," rarely saying anything about the bad weather. Englanders always seem surprised when the weather is good enough to go out of doors, but the old people are always suspicious and say, "Yes, very fine, but too good to last." And the papers write almost as much about it as they do of football and cricket, and go back years to find another day that was as good. (*ICS*, 43)

This kind of reduction by logic of typical English habits to absurdity by the foreigner, viewing everything mouth agape, is Blackburn's stock ploy in *I Came and Saw*. The British customs which come in for the Sarel scrutiny are legion.

Sixpence is likewise alarmed and fascinated. As Sarel records:

For the first few weeks in London I tried hard to shut the boy's eye to the strange ways of Englanders, but he was so wide-eyed that it became useless.

The first thing he noticed on coming to land was the white men working on the roads. . . . I dared not confess to him that white men in England had sunk so deep as to work like the lowest Kafirs without shame, so I told him they were white men being punished for not making their Kafirs work for them. . . . It is all the more horrible and humiliating because the natives will now know that the Englanders who are masters of my country are no better than Kafirs, seeing that they do Kafirs' work. (*ICS*, 47–48)

Bob, Sarel, and Sixpence establish themselves in a salubrious London hotel, the main arena of action for the rest of the novel. There Bob hires a stenographer, one Elsie, and sets up the Rand Diamond Mine Company. At Sarel's suggestion the name is changed to attract more moral investors, and duly the Humanitarian Diamond Company, to be mined on Christian principles, is opened for share subscription. Soon their headquarters fairly buzzes with the landed gentry on the cadge, the socialites out to make a fast pound, the remittance men after cushy jobs, and the clergy as well, avid to invest in philanthropy plus 5 percent (Rhodes's formula for the colonial enterprise). Two special features are the adventuresses out for fortunes, and the charitable organizations in search of patronage. So loudly does the reputation of endless financial resources speak in Blackburn's London that Bob and his crew are the guests of the highest social circles. Accordingly, their rip-offs net in satisfactorily large amounts of capital. It seems to be a society interested only in money, and in making it faster than before. Churchmen, it seems, are able to sanctify the process and benefit from this rush for minerals faster than any others, and Sarel himself, always a petty conniver, is frankly shocked at the stampede Bob's presence causes.

Coupled with this stampede for money is the matrimonial stakes. Both Bob Magnus and Sixpence are unmarried, and Sarel himself is to all intents and purposes an eligible bachelor, at least in the eyes of British womanhood—he never mentions Katrina back home, and has no communication with her. As we know from his previous adventures, Sarel is also chronically woman-shy. Blackburn makes much of this, going as far in his author's note to say:

The ludicrous constraint and timidity in the presence of strange women which is a marked characteristic of the male Colonial, both Briton and Boer, is largely accounted for by the disproportion of the sexes in the Transvaal and Natal, where the preponderance of bachelors is probably greater than in any civilised community. One of the natural results is the exaltation and dominance of the female. This vague "woman fear" often continues far into life, increasing rather than diminishing with years. (*ICS*, viii)

Basically, Bob, Sarel, and Sixpence have to contend with three types of women: in Bob's case it is the wealthy siren in search of a windfall, in Sarel's it is the shrinking violet in search of a man to care for her. In Sixpence's case, in a running drama played out in the basement of the kitchen, it is the Cockney maids of the hotel, who pride themselves on walking out with a "gentleman of colour," a self-proclaimed African prince at that. These three contests interweave with the financial theme, as Mrs. Vavasour a social vamp, Elsie the secretary, and the unnamed cook have basically the same motives for wanting their respective men—the glamour and status of showy money.

It goes without saying that in this treacherous Blackburn world the women win most of the rounds of the courtship contest hands down. After desperately pursuing Mrs. Vavasour, to the extent of buying himself a baronetcy and funding her wastrel son by a previous marriage, Bob, considerably milked of his gains, is in fact turned down by her. As a result, he settles for Elsie, the perfect match for a lover of boxing contests, brandy, and cigars. For Sarel the whole sequence of amorous adventures is excruciating. Without being able to tell the reader in so many words, it is apparent how he yearns for Elsie, with whom he is constantly cloistered in the work situation. The saddest sequence of the novel is his bare account of Elsie's happiness at Bob's hands as he, Sarel, resolves to return to Katrina, his chocolate-guzzling amazon of a wife. Sixpence is finally left behind in England with the cook, and, turning his losses into gains, his wife manning the gate, is last heard of in a circus freakshow as the Wild Man from Gogo.[19]

The novel has three great set-pieces—Sarel's riding out, Bob's banquet, and Elsie's debut as an actress—three of the funniest sequences Blackburn ever wrote. The first of these, Sarel's ride, is worth dwelling on in some detail, because here Blackburn dramatizes the differences between Briton and Boer to greatest effect. The chapter is number 11, subtitled "I revel in the freedom of the English veld."

At a point of disillusion, even despair, over his accumulating financial losses in London, Sarel resolves to carry out

an oft-made plan of getting into the saddle and wandering into the English veld; for there is nothing so good for calming the mind and body as the sleep that comes after many hours in the veld.
I had already found where horses were to be hired; so I tied up some tobacco, cheese, and biscuits in a handkerchief in case I should lose my way and have to sleep out, away from any farmhouse, and went to the place where they let out horses. . . .
When I asked the man how far off was the veld, he seemed very puzzled and asked if it was a public-house, after the manner of certain Englanders who always direct you to a place by saying it is just before, or just after, you come to the "Crown" or the "White Horse," thus showing their drinking habits and customs which they import with them to my land. . . . (*ICS*, 167–68)

When Sarel eventually arrives at something of a piece of open countryside, after endless rows of tenements, and having met no other horse-borne fellow traveler apart from a mounted policeman, he is amazed at the results of European attitudes to property:

wherever there was a gateway leading to what looked like a nice homestead would be a board saying "Private Road," or "Trespassers will be Prosecuted."
They are marvellous people for shutting themselves in and keeping others out, are these Englanders. The real reason is that there are so many thieves among them that they are obliged to make their houses like prisons or forts. (*ICS*, 170–71)

Sarel's broadside potshots like these, made in a state of incredulous wonder, are beguiling for their very probity. He has no understanding of the European system of private land tenure and fencing, nor wants to have one.

Similarly, he is shocked by the class system as it affects the rural unemployed:

Whenever I met men who looked like workers on farms, and even respectable people, they all touched their hats, saying "Good day, sir," but they did not pay any attention to those who walked or drove in carts.
I passed several rough-looking and very dirty men and women carrying small bundles. Some of them stopped to ask for a match and then tobacco.

They were all travelling about looking for work, and had been without food for many days, being what they call on tramp, which is in reality trekking on foot. They explained that even if they found work, which was hard to get, they could not take it, as their tools were in pawn, and they had not the money to redeem them. (*ICS*, 177)

Within an hour of this Hardyesque insight into the lot of the laborers, Sarel is run in, and for an act of unintentional trespass. Thanks to dismounting to climb a hillock to try and achieve a view of fair England, and thanks to hobbling his horse at the base, Transvaal style, he is arrested for suspected poaching, and for cruelty to his mount. Duly bewildered, Sarel remarks: "Knowing that in this land of the free trespass is a crime of very serious proportions, I resisted my desire to make sarcastic remarks or comments of any kind, and accompanied the constable to the police station. . ." (*ICS*, 181).

Elsie rescues him, and here is Sarel describing his joy at reencountering her:

when a man of thirty-nine as intelligent as myself has long been married to a big, fat woman who talks and thinks of nothing but oxen and her quarrels with other women and her Kafir servants, and aggravates this by wearing the same frock day and night for a year, he cannot but be strangely happy when a beautiful young maiden like Elsie, who looks as if she has just come out of a coloured picture postcard, not only shows that she loves him, but comes to comfort him in prison, paying her own railway fare. (*ICS*, 195)

Yet, no sooner than Sarel is sprung from prison, he falls foul of British law once again, in a most spectacular way:

I recovered the mare, and mounted, showing Elsie for the first time in her life proper riding. She walked along the road, admiring me very much, but as she could not walk as fast as I rode she got on a tramcar and I followed it—she going outside so that she could see me. As we got nearer the heart of London the streets began to get more crowded, and I made slow progress, while the tramcar travelled with surprising swiftness, so that I had to gallop to catch it up. During one of these congestions of traffic I had to stop, and the car got so far in front that it was only by hard riding I could come up with it. So I let the mare go at her best, the people scattering away or stopping to stare at the most wonderful sight in London—a man who knows how to ride.

Presently I noticed a mounted policeman in front who stopped and held up his hand, as I thought, in salute. I saluted in response, and was galloping past him when he came by my side and, seizing my bridle, was soon taking me off to the police station, where he charged me with furious riding to the danger of the public. (*ICS*, 200–201)

Once Sarel is again released, he concludes that his six hour expedition on horseback has caused him more trouble "than a troop of Basuto ponies would find for me in a lifetime" (*ICS*, 204). And with remarkable temperance, he concludes: "It is no longer a matter of surprise to me that so many Englanders who come to my land cannot ride. The police and the silly laws of their country are against their using the only sensible means of passing over the face of the earth" (*ICS*, 204). Here Blackburn is celebrating far more than the clash of misunderstanding between Boer and Briton; he is writing a wistful elegy of rural modes of transport as megalopolis and its inventions takes over.

The second set-piece—Bob's banquet for the subscribers to the Humanitarian Mine—is far less gently done; it is a travesty of a company meeting for its shareholders. Bob hires a phony lord to preside, a choir to sing patriotic hymns, jewelry, and a silver dinner service which is to be returned after the ceremony. The occasion is rigged to appear a benevolent Christian organization's presentation to Genial Bob, in reward for his lavish philanthropic works. The ceremony reveals Bob reeling drunk on whisky contained in a jug of milk, Sarel telling the truth that Humanitarian Diamonds have no more than an option on a claim in an area of the Transvaal which never had, and never would, produce diamonds, and Sixpence, beaming in his penguin suit, guzzling all the subscription food.

But what Blackburn calls the "new journalism" (*ICS*, 236) reports the event in the following type of sanctimonious rhetoric, given by Sarel verbatim:

In these days of sordid materialism it is cheering to be able to find an assembly like the present of noble men who do not regard the mission of life to be the laying up of treasure on earth . . . for the first time in the history of joint-stock enterprises [Mr. Robert Magnus] has made the gain of the shareholders subordinate to the interest of the native employees . . . for the benevolent extension of the privileges of civilisation to the fellow countrymen of Sixpence, whom I am proud to see here among us this evening, symbol of that boast of all Englishmen that in this land of the free we know no difference of race, creed, or color. (*ICS,* 110–11)

What in fact is proposed at this launching of this new style of mine is the infamous compound system of barbed-wire enclosures, in which mineworkers on contract are kept for long periods without contact with the outside world. Fatuously, the board of the mine deduces that, if they encourage the mine workers in the wearing of trousers with pockets, they will become thrifty. Curtailing their liberty in virtual concentration camps is similarly justified as obliging them to forego the wicked ways of the city and its vice-infested shebeens. (As Blackburn would show in *Leaven,* his indictment of the compound system, compounding merely pays higher dividends, as workers' earnings are perforce circulated on mine property.) For Sunday relaxation for the miners, the proposal continues, there is always hymn-singing and Bible stories.

Sarel's own account of the proceedings reveals not only his own inability to confront such social controls, but he irrationally blames such abuses on the very man who is to be abused most, Sixpence. One of the running gags of the novel is that every time Sarel catches Sixpence on a platform, being doted over by missionaries and social workers, he grabs up his sjambok and flogs him in public for being so gullible. For this, the other half of the gag goes, Sarel is immediately clubbed into unconsciousness by handbag-wielding, missionary-supporting spinsters, irate at such a display of the slave-holding mentality.

The third set-piece involves Elsie and her coming to stardom, thanks to the doting attentions of Genial Bob, as an actress. In describing Bob's venture into theater patronage, Sarel pulls all the threads of the satire together. By the time Bob's theater manager and his public relations team mount a spectacular piece, which drains a considerable amount of Bob's Humanitarian fortune, Sarel has come into touch with all types and sizes of British society: the lay-about pub-crawlers, the press hounds, the vendors of costumes and scenery, the pawnbrokers and ratty performers. Suffice it to say, the commissioned piece is as elaborate and expensive as the opulent world of London demands, and its only merit, artistic or otherwise, is that it is superbly publicized. Sarel now encounters the center of the British Empire at its most foppish, valueless, and opportunistic.

Blackburn's intention in moving the action into show business circles for the culminating sequence of his Sarel Erasmus cycle is subtle and rewarding. Much of Sarel's knowledge of "home" life is derived from his reading of the popular works of the day and its drama, as was the knowledge of many a colonial—London to the overseas subject was a matter of colored postcards, illustrated magazines, the theater and opera, with its attendant social round and high-life. None of these forms appears to have mirrored the poverty, the unemployment, the housing shortages—in short, the real daily problems of the average citizen—so that Sarel's disillusion over British society is seen and felt by the reader in terms of the popular images of the press and the printer. In the romantic high society drama of Edwardian theater, Sarel is disabused of most of his media-fed illusions.

Elsie changes her name for the play, for example, to Vera Vanessa, the darling of soap advertisements and the endorser of fashionable social spots:

The great trouble came in fixing on a play that would suit Vera. She wanted to be Mary Queen of Scots, because she looked beautiful, with her hair, in a black velvet frock, with a high-standing collar of pearls. Then she wanted in the next act to be a Christian maiden, with very few clothes on except what are used by English women for sleeping in, being thrown to lions and saved by a handsome young actor whom she had insisted should be engaged at a big salary. The last act was to be a ball-room at Park Lane, where she was to dance in the loveliest frock thinkable.

The trouble was to make these very different characters fit into the play, which caused the author great perturbation. . . . Vera was firm, and had ordered the dresses, so there was no help for it but for the author to alter his play to fit the frocks. (*ICS,* 342)

The eventual first night of this appalling costume drama—at the Feathers Theater in the West End—is a disastrous critical failure. But it is Sarel who inadvertently engineers its outrageous success. It happens that one night the foolish Sixpence, supposedly under the spell of the drama, leaps from a box to rescue Elsie as Mary Queen of Scots from the executioner's blade. He and Elsie then dramatically elope, but after a chase through London they are detected and prevented from marrying in the nick of time. The play is adjusted, with Sixpence now written in as Mary Queen of Scots's lover, to satisfy the gossip-mongers. Sarel himself now falls for the illusion of the spectacle, leaping on to the stage in turn to punish Sixpence for pawing over the woman Sarel loves. The sjambok-wielding Boer bigot (actually a disappointed lover) draws the greatest buzz of scandal yet, and the play runs for months to sold-out attendances.

Painfully, Sarel comes to see that he is but a pawn in the clever power game played to huge financial advantage by Bob. The culminating scene of the novel has a fight between them, which is resolved only by Elsie making him swear not to disclose the truth about Bob's entrepreneurial past, his criminal record, and his rise to fame and fortune. Sarel, in the interests of not hurting Elsie, agrees. The Humanitarian mining interest then clears out of England back to the Rand with a fortune in tow, Elsie the manager of Bob's new empire, and a sad Sarel, his meager earnings intact.

What they have left behind is the confirmed image that British business enterprise in foreign parts is an ennobling venture, and that the Boer, though barbarous in race relations, is a distinct asset when inspanned into the colonial enterprise. Nowhere—except perhaps in Blackburn's novel—is the truth told, that Edwardian society is immorally implicated in the extensive exploitation of other peoples, and that the pious virtues and slogans of the time are, in fact, alive only in the hearts of its enemies. The final impact of *I Came and Saw* is thus a somber and chastening one. It records with relish the incongruous hypocrisies of the first decade of the present century, as witnessed by our guileless simpleton, the Burgher hero with an empty pocket and a heart of gold.

It is also a somewhat somber fact that Blackburn's *I Came and Saw* of 1908 did not catch on. It received no critical reception of any note, nor has it remained in print, or even on the shelves of Africana collections in any prominent way. It is one of Blackburn's lost works; its failure in these terms seems to bear no relation to the skill with which it was written, or the intrinsic interest of the work as a pioneering document of South African, or indeed colonial, fiction.

I Came and Saw is both a worthy and a surprising conclusion to the Sarel Erasmus trilogy. The impetus to write this third work in the hand of Sarel Erasmus presumably came to Blackburn on his return to Britain in 1906. In a letter to Blackwood's of March 20 that year, Blackburn requested of the Edinburgh publishing house the return of a manuscript which had the working title *A Study in*

Anarchy, which he had sent them three years previously. He mentions that he is back in England as a result of a costly seven month illness, for an operation on his kidney "for the removal of a bullet I got at the battle of Pieter's Hill" (*EiA,* 43). Whether or not this is another piece of Blackburn blarney we shall probably never know, but the fact of the case is that he spent several months—from at least March to the end of September—of 1906 revisiting the hub of Great Britain, living on the royalties *A Burgher Quixote* had earned him. This return visit, after some fifteen years out of his home country, must have made a distinct impact on him. There would be a reasonable case to be made if we were to compare the wide-eyed Sarel, who bled for his republic, with Blackburn himself, the late Victorian, hand-to-mouth journalist who had also bled for his republic, if symbolically only. We can imagine Blackburn aghast at the changes in London since the days of Victorian solemnity, now frothing with the extravagant high spirits of the Edwardian age, so different from his days at Brighton twenty-five years before.

I Came and Saw was probably completed after sober reflection on his return to South Africa at the end of the year. Having had the *Study in Anarchy* rejected by Blackwood's, he was obviously not likely to submit to them the follow-up of *A Burgher Quixote,* no matter how successful that work had been for them and for him. His letters to Blackwood's of this period are distinctly cool; they are tactfully worded appeals for money due to him, and for an end to the relationship. Here we must speculate, since the actuality is that *I Came and Saw* came out with two other Blackburn works only in 1908—a reprint of *Prinsloo of Prinsloosdorp* and that same *Study in Anarchy,* expanded from a story into a novel and retitled *Leaven*—in the Colonial Library of Alston Rivers, Ltd. The relationship with Blackwood's must have terminated before the completion of *I Came and Saw* and the Rivers agreement been in view, because Sarel himself is frequently given to puffing himself as the author of *Prinsloo of Prinsloosdorp* in the text of *I Came and Saw,* and nowhere does he make a trace of the slightest allusion to his being the author of *A Burgher Quixote* as well. Thus, it seems certain that Blackburn knew that *I Came and Saw* would draw attention to the *Prinsloo* reprint, and vice versa.

In London in 1906 he picked up much free-lance work as a journalist, possibly to augment his earnings in view of his hospitalization. He contributed prominently to *Chambers's Journal* once more and to other publications like the *Wide World Magazine*[20] on his pet subjects, stories of the old Transvaal. Some of these extravagant tales would not disgrace the ingenious Sarel himself. But, as for Sarel, Britain was not Blackburn's true home. His encountering British life again after such a remove, and from such a detached, even cut-off, viewpoint, can only have led to the kind of calculated assessment that is *I Came and Saw*.

This unillusioned scrutiny comes up with some surprising inconsistencies. For one, the military bent of Christianity: "had I not made up my mind to refuse to look at evidence in support of things I had determined not to believe, I should have gone to St Paul's Cathedral to see if it is true, as alleged, that the Temple of the Prince of Peace is full of monuments and praisings of men whose lives have been spent in killing people" (*ICS*, 398).[21] For another, "the English custom . . . of praising work and abusing men who do none, yet all the time striving hard to make money, so that they shall do no more labor, but live in a house in the country as we Boers do, though they call us lazy for doing it" (*ICS*, 398).

In conclusion, Sarel and Blackburn have this to say about the means of achieving parity between motherland and colony:

So long as Englanders can play football and cricket, and bet on horse races, they are not likely to trouble about fighting. The greatest thing we South Africans ever did was to teach Englanders football, by sending a team to show them how the game should be properly played. Since then they have taken to it almost universally, and if they continue to progress at the rate they are going we shall never have occasion to fear another war, for no true Englander would volunteer to go away to fight during the football season, while the summer brings cricket, which is nearly as much a solemn ceremony as football.

Therefore, out of the sport madness of Englanders will come Universal Peace and Brotherhood. (*ICS*, 401–2)

In summing up the range and the richness of the whole Sarel Erasmus cycle, we could not do better than to quote Blackburn himself in his preface to the new edition of the first of the trilogy, in the Rivers reissue of April 1908, the controversial, sharp, and sweet "biography" of Piet Prinsloo, written by his autodidact son-in-law, later chronicler of the South African War, and of the British dispensation of the ensuing decade: "Barely ten years have passed since the first appearance of this little volume, yet during that short period the conditions it describes have ceased to exist, and are already indistinct in the haze of history. Probably in another decade that history will have become allied to myth. . . ."

It is to Blackburn's enduring credit that, in the monumental Sarel Erasmus trilogy, that dramatic decade of accelerated change found its ablest and most endearing recorder. What for us is mere myth, lost in a near-forgotten history, remains living, entertaining, and heartbreakingly real in the presence of Blackburn's magnanimous, naive witness of those days. There is no other novelist who has left such a comprehensive and such an inside view of the decade that shaped modern South Africa.

Chapter Four
Love and Labor: Last Statements

If the Sarel Erasmus trilogy is Blackburn's record of the Boer-British struggle, and *A Burgher Quixote* within this sequence a masterpiece, any claim to his having written a second masterpiece must be based on the evidence of *Leaven: A Black and White Story*. And it deals with the other great issue of South African affairs, the relationship between indigenous and colonizing peoples.

Although certainly first drafted before *I Came and Saw*, during Blackburn's days in the Loteni Valley in 1900–1902—this is the manuscript that started as a short work called *A Study in Anarchy*—and dealing with prewar days, it is convenient to study *Leaven* together with Blackburn's seventh and last novel, *Love Muti*, first published in 1915. Both books deal with the colonial situation in Natal, and both have a common approach to fictional subject matter. Both *Leaven* and *Love Muti* are written in the third person, in a calculatedly antiromantic style. Furthermore, in both of these last "antiromances" Blackburn changes his way of writing from the satirical jibing of farce into a reasonably solemn style that, while still retaining his most typical feature—the accumulation of a driving ironic force—is devoid of the old easy laughs. Both *Leaven* and *Love Muti* appear, at first sight, to be uncharacteristic of the Blackburn we know; they are brooding and dark works, charged with a pessimistic, tragic intensity.

Leaven

When in 1908 Alston Rivers, in his second year as a publisher, issued *Leaven: A Black and White Story* in hardback at six shillings, it received prominent advertising in his list of announcements, and was described by the firm as follows:

The author of *Prinsloo of Prinsloosdorp* has more than once proved his ability to write a sustained and serious story, and though certain aspects of life in South Africa are so absurd as to be merely amusing, there is no question that the native problem with which he has chosen to deal in his latest book is sufficiently grave. So far the Kafir in fiction has either been a farcical chatterbox or an object lesson in futile humanitarianism. Witty and pathetic as Mr Douglas Blackburn can be on occasion, he indulges in neither low comedy, nor sickly sentimentality in *Leaven*. He traces the young Kafir from leaving his native kraal in guilty haste, to the luxury of a good position in a mining compound. Incidentally young Bulalie is cast into prison and treated with the grossest brutality, and the characters who are concerned in his abasement and rescue are altogether original; the unconventional missionary, the Pietermaritzburg landlady, and the compound manager are only a few of the admirable sketches which make *Leaven* a novel of remarkable insight and merit.[1]

Unlike many publishers' blurbs, this description is remarkably accurate. *Leaven* does indeed present the first portrait of a black character in South African literature that does not make him a "farcical chatterbox," etc. In *Leaven* the story of Bulalie from kraal to grave is told with accumulating nuances that make it a work of quite exceptional, realist impact. Of all Blackburn's works, as well, *Leaven* is the one which has dated least, the one which still retains the immediate sting of relevance in the area of labor relationships, where the system Blackburn describes in such thorough detail has hardly changed in South Africa.

The plot of *Leaven* is relatively clean-cut, unencumbered with side issues. It would seem that Blackburn wished to make his case as clear and as direct as possible, by honing the novel form down to having the speed and power which some of his previous, more discursive fiction lacks. In *Leaven* Blackburn exchanges his earlier, more genial technique of fertile comic elaboration for the sparsity and bluntness of polemic in the tragic vein.

The story of Bulalie is obvious enough. We first encounter him at the age of sixteen, at the fringes of his Zulu kraal, almost beyond the reaches of white civilization. He is on guard for a party of police who might be hunting his father down for sheep stealing. The collaring of a stray sheep has been done to celebrate the return home to the kraal of a cousin, a man who beguiles Bulalie with the seductive charm of his proudest acquisition, a concertina. Bulalie is forbidden by his father to leave the kraal for the white man's world on the grounds of his own experience with Natal law—three sentences to flogging, the scars of which are across his back. The family prohibition breaks down almost instantly, as Bulalie's cousin has also introduced rum into the village. When in a flash of drunken rage Bulalie's father assaults him for wanting to leave and seek his fortune, Bulalie kills him with a cooking pot and, an unwilling parricide, takes to the road. Here his picaresque induction into the world beyond his rural idyll begins.

Facing starvation, Bulalie offers himself for work on a road gang. During the course of road building, he falls in with a fellow laborer returned from the diamond mines, who, dying of tuberculosis, entrusts to Bulalie a large diamond which he has secreted away on behalf of his earlier boss. In the event of his friend's death, Bulalie is to endeavor to return it to its rightful owner, and tell him where the rest of his fortune remains hidden. (This, incidentally, is also a good part of the plot of a similar novel of 1929, Frank Brownlee's *Cattle Thief.*) With the arrival of the Natal Mounted Police in search of sheep stealers, Bulalie and friend defect from the road gang and make their way to Pietermaritzburg, the alluring white city. There, with a falsified pass, Bulalie enters employment in a seedy boardinghouse as a general factotum.

The second episode of Bulalie's rise to fortune involves a good part of colonial society and the vices of urban life, but is focused particularly on his encounter with Mrs. Hopgood, his employer. The guileless Bulalie reveals the secret of the diamond to her pet servant, and Mrs. Hopgood moves in. On the pretext of holding the diamond in safe keeping for Bulalie, she in fact steals it. When Bulalie knocks on her door to reclaim the stone, she adroitly switches his timid request into a moral panic of huge dimensions, screams that she is being sexually assaulted, and has Bulalie arrested for attempted rape. In due course, thanks to a crooked lawyer who misadvises him about legal procedure, Bulalie is sentenced to imprisonment for assault upon a reputable white woman and, like his father before him, is to be flogged at the triangle.[2]

On his eventual escape, Bulalie works with a typical outsider figure, a wandering prospector, who in due course introduces him as the ideal material for conversion to a Nonconformist missionary, one David Hyslop, at a station not far from Bulalie's home kraal. Here Bulalie learns writing and arithmetic, the rudiments of the Bible, and becomes Hyslop's sole convert, apart from a rather pathetic outcast from the local tribe, a girl named Anna. Thus is Bulalie "Christianized," as the colonists express it. For a time Bulalie proves Hyslop's able and successful amanuensis and right-hand man.

However, Bulalie soon falls into debt with the local trading store, as do many of his fellows, Christian or no. Hyslop has his arm twisted by a visiting blackbirder, or labor recruiter, into releasing Bulalie, on the grounds that it would not go well with the church if it were to get about that he was harboring an escaped convict. Bulalie is marched off to the Transvaal gold mines, to make up the numbers of a consignment, without having any choice in the matter. He undertakes to remain in touch with Hyslop and to send him his earnings for the purchase of cattle, an investment toward his future return to his home kraal with "bride price" and a concertina.

In the hands of the New Yankee Gold Mining Co., Ltd., and its skillful compound manager, Sid Dane, Bulalie with his superior education soon prospers. Within a short time he is able to cable Hyslop £130 in cash, no mean feat on a salary of fifty-seven shillings per month. Bulalie is appointed "boss-boy" of Dane's compound, and with great application builds his fortune by smuggling liquor into the compound, despite the relative strictness of the liquor prohibition of the period (1896–99), and by loaning money at high interest rates.

These dramatic gains persuade Hyslop that his convert must be acting illicitly and, with the illness of his child as a pretext, he despatches his wife back to the home country, deserts his station, and moves to the Witwatersrand to investigate his convert's fidelity to the Christian creed. Their reunion on the side of a mine dump is a poignant one, as hopeful missionary and noble "native," well learned in the white man's industrial ways, face one another. It becomes Hyslop's personal quest to dissuade Bulalie from his new way of life, and Bulalie's to avoid Hyslop at all costs. So Hyslop becomes a one-man reformist mission to the mines, and the novel is their joint case history.

Eventually, conditions brew up, at the touch of Hyslop's misguided interference, into a faction fight between the employees of the New Yankee and those of a neighboring mine. Hyslop is viciously attacked by liquor runners in the midst of this outbreak, and not he, but Bulalie, is cut down in trying to quell it, as Bulalie makes a dash to pull him out of trouble.

The last scene of the novel takes place in the mine hospital where Bulalie, with a broken back, confesses to his daemon, Hyslop, his original parricide, and the reasons and motives for his subsequent life. Although he sacrifices his life for Hyslop, Blackburn neither indulges in a final recantation, nor in any overworking of his proto-Christian symbolism. Bulalie is another martyr for Christ, who dies resignedly happy in his enduring belief that there is no life after death—he wishes in death to reencounter neither his late father nor the Natal police.

Hyslop is the heir to Bulalie's diamond tale, and to his fortune. The novel ends with his intending to rectify some of the past and, at least, to spring from jail Bulalie's cousin, sentenced as guilty in the case held over Bulalie's father's murder. Through Hyslop the whereabouts of the diamond cache, which Bulalie was to reveal to his friend's former employer, is revealed to its rightful, drunken owner. But the tying-up of the threads of the narrative is left incomplete—no redress for the crimes committed against Bulalie is ever thought of, and it does not occur to Hyslop to tackle the appalling Mrs. Hopgood. Somewhat broken by the truth of Bulalie's revelations, however, Hyslop turns back to proselytizing, sublimely unaware of the personal havoc he has caused in the life of that distant kraal, beyond the pale of the civilizing process.

As is clear from the above summary, *Leaven* is a novel with a double plot. The "raw native" and the optimistic missionary are both caught up in the momentum of a social process which is greater than themselves. The novel is constructed accordingly. The storytelling alternates more or less symmetrically between the stages of the Bulalie story and the stages of the Hyslop story, the latter of which is told in almost as great detail as the former.

David Hyslop himself comes to Natal Colony in those prewar days as a "raw," untested missionary, full of idealistic zeal of the Exeter Hall brand, a favorite target of the colonial novelist averse to liberal high-handedness and to the impracticalness of the holier-than-thou attitudes which, supposedly, had emanated from the meeting place of Exeter Hall since the days of the antislavery lobby and the founding of the Aborigines' Protection Society in mid-Victorian England. Blackburn has like amounts of sympathy for his ill-equipped protagonist and of scorn for the implications of his unsuitability in handling his job. Hyslop's own story proceeds in well-marked stages—his settling in to a derelict mission post; his well-meaning attempts to preach to and to convert the heathen; his loneliness as he becomes an outcast in white colonial society; his battle with the Natal press who mercilessly rag him under the nickname of the "Kafir Disintegrator"; his mirthless marrying of a zealous governess and their progress with the imbecilic Anna; his crisis of faith in pursuing Bulalie to the Rand; his investigations there as a free-range priest intent on tackling the mine moguls single-handedly; and his final resolution to continue in his work, despite his manifest defeat on both the commercial and the spiritual levels. Hyslop's progress goes through as many gradations as Bulalie's, and the essence of the novel lies in the interplay between the two plots as they develop to one end.

Seldom has a writer, working with South African material, thrown together a more incongruous pair of main characters. Bulalie, one of nature's gentlemen, with his fine physique and sparkling teeth— Blackburn is particularly clever at using the clichéd portrait of a black man against the stereotype—and the red-cheeked, apple-fresh priest are equally uneducated in the exigencies of living in an industrializing world. It would be correct to say that *Leaven* is yet another variation on a well-tried Blackburn formula, but the incongruities and contrasts of this double disabusement of two unlikely, interdependent innocents is both more far-reaching, and more daring, than anything Blackburn had tried before.

In *Leaven* this double perspective is held in control by an unfalteringly objective narrative voice. The feat of ventriloquism that is the Sarel Erasmus saga is nowhere in evidence here, nor are the fanciful twists of language that give Blackburn's impersonations such convincing authenticity. *Leaven* is a singularly "uncharming" work. It uses a dry, clinical style. It is not, however, devoid of comedy, in the best Blackburn manner, as the story does frequently erupt into humor. But humor, in *Leaven,* is not used cathartically to explode follies and fancies, as in Blackburn's satirical work, but to underscore passages of horror. Also, it is used so sparingly, and with such abruptness, that it serves to intensify the mood of angry despair which pervades the work.

The leaven of the title is explained in the epigraph to the novel— "It is like the leaven which a woman took and hid in three measures of meal till the whole was leavened"—from St. Luke's Gospel. Metaphorically, Blackburn means by leaven the power of righteousness and justice to alleviate the situation in which the characters find themselves. *Leaven* is Blackburn's most obviously moralizing work, moralizing in the sense that moral issues are quite plainly drawn for the reader's cogitation. However, it is never at fault for the issues it raises not being integrally related to the dramatic development of the characters participating in the drama. Many of these issues are familiar to us from other Blackburn works: the damaging influence of liquor on the social fabric of preindustrial societies, the wholesale injustice of the courts which prefer white claims to black evidence, the rebarbative prison system, the bondage into which a man falls in an economic system designed to exploit rather than elevate him, and so on. But in *Leaven* he is more concerned with the prewar labor recruitment system as it operated in a British sphere of influence like Natal (despite the fact that recruiting for the mines was illegal in the colony), and in the role the state church plays in sanctioning malpractices. The latter part of this theme is new in Blackburn's novels, having been only partially treated in *I Came and Saw*. In making one of his two main characters in *Leaven* a clergyman, Blackburn brings the whole issue of the Christian onslaught on heathendom right out into the light of day, and relates it to the spiritual condition of British colonial life in general. Like *I Came and Saw*, *Leaven* is also based on a profound reversal of the norms of colonial fiction of the time—in the former the conquered visits and judges the conqueror, and now we have the heathen sitting in judgment on the Christian. Although *Leaven* deals entirely with events before the South African War, and thus feels as if it is a far earlier work than *I Came and Saw*, at this level of ideation it is, indeed, a later and maturer work.

The seeds of the *Leaven* story date back a long way, as do many of the original concepts that underlie Blackburn novels. They derive from the ebullient time of his one-man newspaper crusades, and were probably planted in his fertile imagination when in the *Transvaal Sentinel* he wrote a column signed by one Slim Ofanzo, entitled "A Kaffir Mission to England":

I talk to my brother as he come from England with his baas. He say white men want missionary much, that they do everything missionary tell Kaffir not to do, and all for want of money. Brother says white baases beat their wives in England same as Kaffir in kraal, and run away with other boys wife as no kaffir do. Also that white man drinks all day Sundays, and go to no church, that is why missionaries come here, having no work to do.

This is very bad, so editor, baas, I want Kaffirs to give money to send a good kaffir boy to Engeland to teach white men to be good. (*TS*, February 23, 1898)

This slim, or artful, use of pidgin to turn the moral tables on the overlord is wielded much more subtly in *Leaven*. We are inevitably led to the moral conclusion that Hyslop at the end of the novel should turn his attentions from the black man back to the masters who sent him out to Africa in the first place; it is not the heathen, but they, who need salvation. The missionary thrust in *Leaven* turns full circle, and in our eyes it is Hyslop who needs the mercy and righteousness of the title.

The fundamental theme of *Leaven,* then, is that there is no escape from the civilizing process—one concertina intruding into rural life is enough to precipitate the full catastrophe of a one-way trip to experience. Axiomatically, civilization neither ennobles nor liberates the black man from his former ways; it reduces him to servitude, loses him his identity, and offers him a life of bare survival only through criminal trespass and evasion of the law. (The same theme endures in South African writing right through to a work of the 1970s like Athol Fugard, John Kani, and Winston Ntshona's play, *Sizwe Bansi is Dead*.) Nor, in Blackburn's view of the situation, is the white man exempt from taking responsibility in this general drift. One of the striking facets of *Leaven* is its foresight in seeing that the reduction to slavery of other "non-European" races recoils on the enslaver.

The following passage of dialogue is between Mr. Fraser, a somewhat principled mine manager, and Hyslop:

"Has it ever occurred to you that association with the black is prejudicial to the white?"
"Some whites, no doubt. But explain."
"It may have occurred to you that the majority of whites in this country are not precisely the type of men one would cite as fair samples of civilisation or Christian manhood."
Mr Hyslop assented with a sad smile.
"These men, finding themselves in authority over a subordinate race, are not likely to exercise that restraint and thoughtful consideration that the strong, righteous man should show to the weak. In other words, they take advantage of their opportunity to assert their instinctive tyranny. . . . The class of men who come to mining camps are not over-

burdened with the finer moralities. They have left their morals at home, and mean to put them on with their dress suits when they go back with a pile. . . ."[3]

This insight into the reciprocal nature of the enslaver-slave bond is remarkable in a novel of the period. It would not be an idle claim to make that Blackburn's *Leaven* is the first South African analysis of labor relations that should be taken with some respect.

There are many such instances of Blackburn's perspicacity in the novel, all of which take us very far from the romantic myths of the conquest of black heathendom so popularized by a figure like H. Rider Haggard. Once again, Blackburn nods at Haggard in a novel: we have seen the "Bulalie link" before. A mere two decades after Haggard—the time of the beginning of the action of *Leaven* is the early 1890s—the romance of African conquest has turned around into becoming Blackburn's parodic antiromance.

This aspect of *Leaven* is also apparent in the Hyslop story. Previously, Blackburn had often based a novel on a pre-existing type of writing, and then inverted it. In both *Richard Hartley, Prospector* and *I Came and Saw* it was the travelogue of the *Weekend in South Africa* strain. This time the pre-existing literature is specifically the missionary pamphlets and reports which Sarel Erasmus read in the Cape Town YMCA, and which David Hyslop brings with him to Africa in his trunk, the very literature which conditioned Victorian and Edwardian thinking about the Dark Continent and the colonial mission. Here is how Blackburn shows up its most basic, rainbow-colored assumptions for what they are:

David Hyslop was saved from mental decadence through finding most of his preconceived ideas challenged by the experience of the days. Instead of coming to teach, he discovered he had first to learn, and in the process, to discard many pleasant prejudices and illusions.

It had taken him the better part of a year to assimilate these stern facts. The process had been painful, for it revealed the state of innocence and inexperience that was his when he permitted his naturally enthusiastic and emotional nature to be swayed by what he then honestly believed to be the call to the mission field. He had dedicated himself to a task whose nature was hidden in the haze of romance. (*L*, 143–44)

At moments of crisis and stock-taking, a symbol recurs for Hyslop, a "bar across the disc of the moon" (*L*, 144), which seems to

Love and Labor: Last Statements 121

be not a crucifix, but an ironically placed hammer and sickle, hinting of the workers' revolution to come. It contrasts sharply with Bulalie's recurring concertina symbol. Yet the "haze of romance" is never fully dispelled from Hyslop, this "ascetic, oval-faced, saint-suggestive person" (*L,* 21). His role in colonial society is predetermined by the nature of his post. His mission station dominates a location, or tribal reserve, of some three hundred square miles (the Loteni District, although not named as such), conquered from its regional chief and given back to him, in exchange for labor, and in exchange for money in the form of hut tax, payable in cash to the missionary himself.

Interestingly, since *Leaven* is partly written at the end of the period of Blackburn's Loteni retreat, we now see him advocating the view that no one, no matter how remote or reclusive, is immune from the social process. Thus, even Hyslop in the back of beyond inherits a system designed to provide a tithe of free labor to Natal Colony, and a system of financial debits and credits devised to hasten the proletarianization of the tribal area. As Blackburn sees it, these intrusions are neither beneficent nor elevating. Of the road gangs he sourly remarks:

> They were merely natives "called out" *nolens volens,* to give one month's service to the Colony of Natal under the law which provides that the native chief who occupies a small slice of land taken from him by his white masters may continue to live on it if, among other tributes and services, he supplies a certain amount of labor for the public roads. The Natal Government is careful to explain that the servitude is not obligatory, for the native "called out" has perfect freedom of contract. He has the alternative choice of working for three months with pick and shovel on the roads for tenpence per diem or for an equal or longer period in preparing road material in the local jail in return for mealie pap and free water. Many of them prefer the alternative after one experience of the free and open life of the road gang. (*L,* 11–12)

The no-choice situation governs mission finances as well. At its most ludicrous extreme, Hyslop finds himself devising a system for his subject folk of attendance at church services as a method of repaying accumulated debts. And one of the principles Hyslop learns the hard way is that even the "Christianized" native is hardly thirsting for doctrinal enlightenment.

Another of Hyslop's disillusions is his relationship with the colonial administration and settlers:

> True, he had received glimmering impressions in his student days that there were godless, selfish persons who took no interest in, and even passively resisted, the great and glorious work of regenerating the heathen; but he knew that, according to the missionary reports, these "obstacles" invariably came to the missionary sooner or later, tearful and penitent, to testify to the change wrought in the native and themselves and to contribute prodigally to the fund for erecting church or mission house. (*L*, 31–32)

In truth, his lone effort is implacably opposed by colonial officials and their white agents. The terms upon which he is to missionize are made clear:

> ". . . rub it into the kafirs that they are to work for the white man. . . . You preach on them lines, and you'll have the farmers agreein' with you. Work at cheap rates is what is wanted, and if religion will bring it, you may count on me for one not to oppose you. You don't know how difficult it is to get boys to work at our price. Rub the Catechism into 'em, about bein' meek and lowly to all their betters, and bein' content in the state o' life to which it has pleased God to call 'em. Teach 'em what the Bible says about their bein' the children of 'Am and bein' under a cuss, and don't forget the dignity of labor. The lazy brutes hate work, and I tell you I quite expect to live to see the day when we farmers and our sons will have to work. . . ." (*L*, 87)

The institutionalized underdevelopment of rural black land for purposes of creating labor reservoirs is something of a shock to Hyslop. A crisis comes for him when he is invited to give a guest sermon on the missionary enterprise in a free-thinking Pietermaritzburg church. The scene is carefully built up and horrific in its implications, for Hyslop, once given the platform, takes off in a stammering, red-faced tirade against his pious white congregation, with helpless and inappropriate effect:

> "I admit that the civilised native is an unattractive object—to those who do not understand him. He is a parody of civilisation, a pathetic specimen of incompleteness, but he is what you white men have made of him, not the missionary.

"You accuse us of teaching the native that he is the equal of the white. If you took the trouble to find out what we do teach, you would know that our one great aim is to warn and prevent the native from imitating most of the whites they meet, because the model is such a bad one." (L, 236)

For Hyslop, his inveighing against the system of which he is a part is a frustrating and fruitless act. In fact, so drastically does he revise his ideas on the black-white question by the end of the novel that he is in favor of radical separatism between the races, of enforcing a system of segregation between the colors that will turn the mines over to white labor and leave the black man to develop along his own lines on his own territory. (The rhetoric of radical separatism bears a marked similarity to the jargon of the apartheid policy of today.) As the only scholar of recent times to examine Blackburn, Isabel Hofmeyr, remarks, the whole of *Leaven* is an endorsement of this separatist ideology which was prevalent before the Union of South Africa, and which became one of the ground principles of racial segregation from that date onwards. Hofmeyr finds *Leaven* an illustration of such thinking, the Bulalie story being the exemplum of the bad effects of inducing blacks into the labor system, and the Hyslop story being the ideological rationale of the development of separatist principles.[4]

This view of the novel is only partially true, although there are persuasive reasons for subscribing to it. Blackburn himself was certainly an advocate of what many of the adherents of the rising science of anthropology named "Kaffir Socialism." In an article for the *New Age,* the London socialist weekly review, published in the same year as *Leaven,* Blackburn came clean on the whole issue, writing the thesis of which *Leaven* can be taken as the illustration:

It is surprising how few of the typical champions of the old order, who denounce all social reforms because it will "disintegrate the integrity of the British Empire" know anything about that Empire beyond their own immediate district. Least of all are they aware that the most stable and contented of the subject races of the Empire are Socialists, and that it is only when they discard Socialism for modern civilisation that they become a source of menace to their white masters.

The natives of South Africa are essentially Socialistic. Their system of life is based on the rudimentary principles of Socialism, and their white lords and masters have encouraged and perpetuated that system unaware of its true nature, but because long experience has convinced them that it is the system best calculated to satisfy both natives and whites.

I am not concerned with tracing and illustrating that affinity beyond its elementary stage. My aim is rather to call attention to a very instructive object-lesson acknowledged by all authorities on native affairs: that so long as the native remains under the aegis of his communism he flourishes in content, but that when so-called modern civilised methods are introduced by way of improvement upon his old conditions of life, the native for the first time manifests those predatory and criminal habits which are fostered by the lust of private possession.[5]

We might well deduce from this that Blackburn was in favor of reversing the flow of the black man to the cities, and to ensure safety for the white population by keeping him at a remove in some distant rural communism. As the tone of radical separatism indicates, the middle years of the first decade of the century was also a time of large-scale rumors of violent native uprisings (the subject of *Love Muti*).

Nevertheless, *Leaven* itself does not entirely endorse segregationist thinking. Hyslop the character does develop that way, and is motivated to change the selective giving of the white man to the black man, on preferential and discriminatory terms, into a rejection of the black man, on the somewhat zany moral grounds that the white gift can only be one of corruption and destruction of black communal values. In the name of preserving some decency among his parishioners, Hyslop is even prepared to denounce his own religion. But what Hyslop takes to be a solution to the problem is not necessarily what Blackburn the novelist is advocating. The novel itself makes a wider statement and, in order for us to see it, we must turn to the Bulalie story.

The truth about Bulalie—and this is the truly extraordinary part of *Leaven*—is that his story is by no means a mere illustration of some social theory of the times. Like all of Blackburn's put-upon characters, Bulalie is an avid learner; no sooner is he manipulated than he learns to turn the manipulation around in his favor. He outgrows the clan, the tribe, and even his blackness in a couple of years of intense experience. Bulalie's story also tells us of the man's real potential. Within a heinously restrictive social system he develops a great capacity for survival. He is thwarted from growing into his own at the end of the novel, as the very forces he has grown beyond accumulate to kill him.

Although Blackburn probably could see no way for Bulalie to survive at that time, the portrait is not merely one of a disabused rural socialist come to the vile city and succumbing. Bulalie is far better able to improvise a survival kit than is Hyslop. Bulalie himself might die in this novel, but Bulalie's type contains the inner resourcefulness and smartness to outlive his master in the end. In this respect *Leaven* is an even more outspoken novel than the famous variation on the theme of "Jim Comes to Joburg," Alan Paton's *Cry, the Beloved Country*. The latter optimistically settles for some kind of working Christian partnership between black and white in the molding of the future of South Africa. Blackburn suspected partnership; he renamed it extortion. He foresaw that Bulalie's children might somehow become the inheritors of a post-Christian, postcapitalist world.

This would seem clear from the unexpected details Blackburn lavishes on Bulalie. Indeed, considering the state of relations between the races at the turn of the century, it is quite shocking to come across a novel which actually extols a black man with care and—dare one say it—with love. Blackburn makes Bulalie a strongly attractive man, fully and sensuously present on the page. For Haggard and his school's gallery of fawning idiots and aggressive grotesques, we now have a delicately waisted, lithe beauty of a man, presented with a homo-erotic intensity. Bulalie's graceful male beauty is created for dramatic effect, to be sure, because Blackburn's main metaphor throughout the work is the brutalizing effect of the white man's law and order. The uglier Bulalie is made by his contact with civilization, the more upsetting is his dilemma to the reader. So obsessive is white control about spoiling Bulalie's loveliness that, on the physical level, the novel often reaches a sadomasochistic intensity, notably in the flagellation scenes in the hands of the law. The disfigurement of Bulalie as the work progresses is also meant to play on the white man's conscience, and the last we see of him, as he expires, is a picture set up like an icon to haunt us: "David Hyslop . . . gently pressed down the lids of the eyes that were fixed upon his, and drew the blanket over the black but comely face" (L, 325).

The depiction of Bulalie as a fine-looking swain also clearly has a polemical value. His beauty relates to the chief symbol of the book, which is incised in gold ink on the Rivers cover of the publication. It is the cat-o'-nine-tails, the instrument of the oppressor's control. Second only to the cat is the sjambok, the "tapering rod of rhinoceros hide, tough and flexible as the gutta percha it resembled" (*L,* 40). Blackburn had previously dealt with flogging as a means of social control (in *Richard Hartley, Prospector*), but in *Leaven* the whip sings with a vileness that makes it revolting.

Society's vengeance on Bulalie is the result of a Black Peril scare caused by his supposedly having attempted to ravish Mrs. Hopgood. The scare panics Pietermaritzburg, and particularly its conservative press, into denunciations of black virility in general, and its threat to innocent white women in particular. The campaign is conducted in torrid, emergency prose: "Outrage!" and so on. As a result, once the medical inspector decides that "the patient was fit for treatment" (*L,* 140), revenge is taken in a most severe manner. Bulalie "had often when bathing in the water hole looked at the reflection of his own smooth, shapely shoulders and wondered if they would ever become disfigured like his father's" (*L,* 127). The treatment begins:

> A tiny clot of flesh and blood flew past and settled on the triangle just where his eyes rested. He looked at it and wondered whether more would come. It must have been pieces like that which came from the back of his father and left those big furrows that he used to put his baby fingers into. Several times he had to clench his teeth and turn his tongue back in his mouth to keep back the scream that was trying so hard to come up, and once he thought he must let it come, not so much because of the agony as from shame and anger, for the water was blinding his eyes; he was shedding big tears as women do. He could hold back the screams no more; it came up, loud and broken and with it, words:
> "Baas, baas, my heart is dead!" Four times more red hot wires twined round his body, then they stopped.
> He turned his head to look over his shoulder, but the water would not let him see. He knew that they were doing something soft and cool, and then came a mountain of stinging, throbbing pain that could not be borne and Bulalie screamed as only strong men do at the triangle.
> They untied his wrists and ankles, pulled on his shirt and led him to the cell. They were very gentle with him, for they knew that only a very small part of the punishment had been borne. . . . (*L,* 141)

This passage brings a point about narration to the fore. While Blackburn rarely has Bulalie speak in English, his point of view permeates the third-person line in many places. Blackburn lets his

Love and Labor: Last Statements

inadequate grasp of English reflect his inability to counteract the system. Rather than rendering Zulu thoughts literally into English, Blackburn slides the narrative into indirect thought with great effect. Writing at this intensity is no mere sensationalism, either. The tone of this passage displays a cold fury. Blackburn wishes to show, in the most controlled detail, the implications of the penal system of his times as it affected one man. And here oppression takes many strange forms, for it is a black warder, no less, who administers the lashing, than whom none could be more vengeful on the white man's behalf.

Now, *Leaven* was the one novel of Blackburn's which drew intense reaction from his supporters, and from his detractors. Hardly a reviewer—and there were many of them—was able to maintain a detached stance toward this controversial work. As Blackburn himself remarked: "You may publicly attack the sanctity of marriage, even the leading tenets of the Christian faith, and be sure of a certain amount of public and influential support and sympathy, but to deprecate missionary enterprise or the right of the black subject to the theoretical privileges of brotherhood would be to raise a storm, to which the extremists of every party in Britain would contribute a blast."[6] In the same piece, in talking about his reporting on the "native question" for "a well-known and influential English journal," he notes: "Again and again my items dealing with the native have been cut or toned down out of recognition. . . ." So, with *Leaven,* Blackburn meant to have his say, and the result was noteworthy.

First, the supporters. Reviewers of a more liberal persuasion were suitably chastened, and even appalled, by the revelations made in *Leaven.* The *Manchester City News* reacted as follows: "*Leaven* deserves a place by the side of *Uncle Tom's Cabin* as one of the gravest indictments of white man's rule that has ever been penned. With a fervor as ardent and a realism as vivid as that of Mrs Beecher Stowe, yet with a restraint which emphasizes its truth, he depicts the native as the victim of cruellest oppression and absolute brutality. . . ."[7]

The *Bookman* in London, which is a fine source of reviews and article material about colonial literature of this period, and which carried a lengthy puff about *Leaven* from Alston Rivers in the August issue of 1908, reviewed it with detailed and empathetic praise:

Four things that become clear to any one reading *Leaven* are that the negro problem in South Africa is one of the most difficult, as well as one of the most momentous, problems of the day; that the brutal methods of treatment in favor with the majority of whites out there are not likely to solve it; that the kindly, humanitarian methods advocated by the minority are even less likely to do so; and that the safety, if not the very existence, of the usurping population depends on its solution. . . .[8]

Many such reviewers of the work who agree with the basic argument made by Blackburn cite the author's "expert" knowledge of labor matters as justification for his case, and their evaluations of the work's merit hence derive from a validation of his expertise.

So partisan were the endorsements reviewers made of *Leaven*, and so accurately had Blackburn managed to work on the consciences of the philanthropists back home, that some praise for the work was even more fulsome. In the generally starchy columns of the *Academy*, assessment of the work glowed with such incandescence that it is hard to imagine how *Leaven* has become so forgotten:

Great are the responsibilities and difficulties of the novelist who attempts a study of the relations between the white and black races, and if he succeeds his triumph is all the more noteworthy. Mr Douglas Blackburn is in the happy position of realising that he has given us the very best novel on South Africa that has yet appeared. *Leaven* is a magnificent story, written with a sense of humour combined with a sense of honour. The author touches upon many of the gravest questions, moral and political; yet it is impossible to tell what his own private opinions are, for this book, though to a certain extent political, is quite unbiased . . . anyone who knows good literature will find it in *Leaven*, even if he is not interested in "South African problems," and that is high praise.[9]

The lack of bias, we may feel, that even maintenance of irony, that resisting of stacking the argument in favor of a rhetorical onslaught, is the root strength of Blackburn's method. It is his great claim to fame as a novelist of the period, able to maintain the even-handedness of reason in the most emotional, explosive areas.

Second, the detractors. Not all British reviewers were as ready to extol the virtues of *Leaven* as a novel, and to ferret through the implications of the narrative with its implied damnation of the labor model. The *Daily Mail* in London, for which Blackburn himself would free-lance from Tonbridge a decade later, was tight-lipped

Love and Labor: Last Statements 129

and dismissive of the work, as it was of any fiction that had the merest echo of the socialist jargon of the times. Homing in on the polemical tone of *Leaven* (which is nowhere in evidence), their reviewer had this to say:

> Mr Blackburn is emphatically a writer with a purpose, and perhaps this otherwise excellent story suffers just a little for that reason. His desire to prove that neither the black nor the white man is improved by contact with the other has probably caused the writer to draw Colonial life somewhat darker than it is. Or, at least, we hope so, for there is not much in this book to make us view with pride the progress of civilisation in South Africa. . . . Does Mr Blackburn suggest what that way should be? We hardly know. He speaks of "leavening," but rather vaguely, and on the whole we are inclined to think that he does not show clearly how the leavening should be done.[10]

We might retort that the image of the leaven, which so subtly underlies the work, and which recurs to unite the structure of the novel at key points of transition, is hardly vaguely placed or used in a wishy-washy fashion. It is used as a motif that provides the novel with density, richness, and pathos, and its accumulative effect is to build an indictment of the unleavened condition of human relations of the day.

Blackburn's detractors generally disallow the work's having a unity of structure and an orderly pattern of imagery at all. They are able to damn the work under the cloak of faint praise, too, while betraying a notion about fiction which is altogether undermining of Blackburn's achievement. They tend to assume that the various elements of the novel are detachable, as if style were not linked to characterization, and characterization to structure, and so on. Thus the *Daily Mail*'s limp conclusion: "Mr Blackburn writes well and draws a number of interesting characters."

Third, the local furore. From the colony of South Africa, and among the "usurping population of Natal" in particular, the work drew an altogether different response, one which is so virulent and so emotional that it is not hard to deduce some very good reasons why Blackburn's work was swept under the carpet (where it remains to this day). *Leaven,* it seems, brought so many issues of conscience to the fore, so weighed the entire system of which the story of Bulalie and Hyslop is but a part, that reaction could well be characterized as hysterical. The description of "Hysteria" was, in fact, applied to Blackburn, and in the most aggressive manner:

> *Leaven: A Black and White Story,* by Douglas Blackburn, will not greatly help either the Kafir's comfort or the author's literary reputation. . . . [It] is an open, loudly-shouted, almost hysterical attack on the Natal Government in particular and South African white men in general, for their treatment of the native. . . .
> Even if Mr Blackburn made out a strong case against the manner in which Natal and the Transvaal administer justice to the native, he does not help us. He gives us a sermon in 328 pages; but he arrives at no conclusion. He tells us (in very feeble language, let it be said) that we are a most abandoned crowd. . . . Nor has his wrongful preference for the novel [as against the sermon] helped his literary methods. His style has never before been so bad. His plot has never been so flimsy. . . . Here there is nothing but an air of utter provinciality, of hysteria, of unreality. . . . On the whole, one has rarely read anything more illogical, more tedious and less literary than *Leaven*. The Natal people may be very bad and all that, but such arguments as those which Mr Blackburn uses are not going to make them better.[11]

To add insult to injury, this reviewer even goes as far as to describe Blackburn as "an invalid who lives in Basutoland." So much for the provinciality of a Cape newspaper in solidarity with the garden colony of Natal, a backwater province to be unruffled by further literary scandal until William Plomer's *Turbott Wolfe* burst forth some eighteen years later.

From Plomer's novel itself we might conveniently take our postscript to the *Leaven* story. When in 1926 Plomer shocked the colonial literary sensibility with his mildly impressionistic and juvenile work, one of his characters had the perfect retort to those who wax weighty on the subject of the "native question," or who divine neurotic tendencies where there is only logic and a simple statement of first principles: "native question! What the hell *is* the native question? You take away the black man's country, and, shirking the future consequences of your action, you blindly affix a label to what you know (and fear) the black man is thinking of you—'the native question' . . . there is no native question. It isn't a question. It's an answer. . . ."[12]

In conclusion, we might well remember that there were some readers of discernment and of taste at the time. They were the ones who found Blackburn's last great work sufficiently successful to pay it the tribute of being "the very best novel on South Africa that has yet appeared."

Love Muti

The subject of Blackburn's last novel, *Love Muti,* is also that "native question," though in a very particular form. Another reference to Plomer's *Turbott Wolfe* is appropriate here; the brunt of the outrage caused by Plomer's novel arose from its theme of mixing and marrying across the color bar—of miscegenation, to give it the pseudoscientific name of the time. In a society dominated by the color line like South Africa, it is inevitable that novelists should concentrate on this issue. The clash between the private loves of individual human beings of different racial groups, and the public taboos against interracial sex, is the ideal terrain for the novelist intent on demonstrating the quality of South African life. As Michael Wade comments, "It is apparently quite obligatory for all South African novelists to try their hand at least once at the theme of miscegenation."[13] Nor is it surprising that this specific type of novel should begin to emerge in the early years of this century, once the domination of South Africa by the British Empire was complete. The new question of how to maintain that dominance, by entrenching the custom of a color bar in law, became the new issue of the day.

Plomer's *Turbott Wolfe* might have brought the issue into the limelight, as it affected the South African English novel, but was by no means the first work to handle this controversial, and even painful, theme of the Immorality Act. Perceval Gibbon's *Souls in Bondage* of 1904 had already touched on the so-called "Colored Question," debating the role of the half-caste in colonial society, and in 1908 the most popular play staged in South African history, Stephen Black's *Love and the Hyphen,* had launched the theme of interracial affairs into the public debate of the theater. In 1911 Gibbon's masterpiece, the novel *Margaret Harding,* technically became the first work of South African fiction which dealt boldly and openly with a cross-ethnic love match. Blackburn's *Love Muti*—which must have been written earlier than the Gibbon—appeared a few years later, with an equally bold scrutiny of the whole issue.

The date of composition of *Love Muti* is hard to determine. The action of the novel takes place during a period of a year or so, the central event being the uprising of the Zulu in Natal against the white population, whom they outnumbered nine to one. This event took place in February 1906, and is known after its unsuccessful leader as the Bambata Rebellion. The uprising is not presented in any great detail in the novel, but in one brief reference is described as follows:

The Zulu rising of 1905, long feared and foretold by some, scouted by others, had come with a suddenness that astonished even those who for weeks had been sleeping with rifle in hand and horse in paddock. Inspector Hunt, of Maritzburg, an adept in official conciliation, had been treacherously assagaied while collecting the native tax that was the *casus belli*, and Natal was up in arms. Police and fighting corps of experienced volunteers had poured into Zululand and the disaffected districts, and an able commandant was striking with a promptitude and effect that justified the Bismarckian axiom—the most ruthless war is in the long run the most humane.[14]

The rebellion cost Natal all of a million pounds in military operations, resulted in over 2,000 Zulu deaths, and dragged on through the wooded, outlying areas of Zululand proper until August 1906, when Chief Dinizulu, son of the great King Cetewayo, was arrested and tried for complicity in the uprising. His trial in turn dragged on into 1908, and was the cause célèbre of the National Convention that sat that year to unite the four provinces of South Africa in 1910. The trial of Dinizulu is the last historical fact mentioned in *Love Muti*.

It was written, then, partly on Blackburn's return to Natal from London in September 1906, and must have been completed, at least in a first draft, by 1908, when he finally left South Africa. It was first published by another of the unsuccessful publishers of Blackburn's day, Everett and Co. of the Strand, London, with no date given, but the date of deposition in the British Museum is March 4, 1915. Why it had to wait for all of seven years before being issued will have to remain a mystery.

Its appearance during the second year of World War I, when the British reading public could not have been less concerned with old colonial troubles, we must take as sufficient reason for the novel's having sunk without trace. There are no reviews of the work, and we are now dealing with the somewhat inglorious finish to a great career.

Of all his works, however, *Love Muti* is one that least deserves such oblivion. World War I itself, which reshaped so many of the attitudes of the modern world, took the older school of Edwardian novelist with it, and Blackburn, like Rudyard Kipling, Thomas Hardy, and even Joseph Conrad, remains, if at all, as a monument to an order that was profoundly changing. *Love Muti* is really about last things.

As ever with Blackburn, the connection between the life he lived and the work itself is something of a puzzle. Before returning to South Africa in 1906 from hospitalization in London, he wrote to Blackwood's as follows:

> I am leaving on Monday [in late September] for S. Africa & hope to return again when the Native War is ended. I have to join my Corps.
> You are right in your suggestion that the present Govmt has muddled S. African matters. I fear we Colonials will have bitter cause to regret the change. The Liberal Party has ever bn the nemesis of S. Africa & if they run counter to Colonial feeling in this case I as a Britisher shall fear for the continuance of Imperialism there. . . . (*EiA*, 44)

We can only interpret this letter as an obscure manifestation of sycophantic behavior. Blackburn himself was never a member of any mounted military corps, was not against the new Liberal government, and had always, as we know, been implacably opposed to the imperial progress. Blackburn was frequently given to such amazing two-facedness in his letters to Blackwood's. In one letter of Christmas Day, 1903, he had similarly fawned over the arch-imperialist writer of the day in South Africa, John Buchan, also a Blackwood's author:

> Just a hurried line to thank you for the copy of Mr Buchan's splendid book. I came down country yesterday and have not yet left the club as the Book fascinates me. I know the North Transvaal which Mr B. describes and am delighted to find it so admirably described. The accuracy and insight are marvellous. I thought I knew that Country,—Mr Buchan can teach me much. Tom Hartley, one of the pioneers of that region, is here. I read him bits. His criticism was to the point: "If that man had come here sooner we shd not have had so many false impressions given of the Country. . . ." As a matter of fact this is the first time that region has been described. I am amazed at the accuracy of detail.[15]

The book referred to is Buchan's *The African Colony: Studies in Reconstruction*, to which Blackburn implicitly replies in his far better book, *Richard Hartley, Prospector*, with drastically different views of affairs. (The real name Hartley suggests the semifictional nature of that novel.)

And now, with *Love Muti*, Blackburn was to see the problems of the 1906–8 rising in a manner quite incompatible with an admiration for a romancer like Buchan. Buchan's version of the identical events, *Prester John*, first appeared in 1910. While *Prester John* deals with the final breaking of the tribes and their admission to the white man's civilization on the white man's terms, *Love Muti* restates the case, and argues it through to very different conclusions. So, once again, we have a work by the cussed Blackburn which goes flat in the face of popular colonizing opinion about Africa. In *Love Muti*, too, the contradictory Blackburn rather shows the British plans for the reconstruction of the postwar South Africa to be shallow, inept, and unlikely to succeed. Like *Leaven*, *Love Muti* is also profoundly an antiromance. To put it crudely, it is not the romantic hero out from Britain who wins in *Love Muti*, but the powers of darkness he is unable to subdue.

The plot of *Love Muti* is the least complex of all Blackburn's inventions. It concerns Charlie Rabson, a listless Englishman in his early twenties, come out to the Colony of Natal to prove himself: "He was about four-and-twenty, fair-skinned, and obviously English and 'newly-out,' for his riding dress was too blatantly 'West End' and his demeanor too easy for him to be mistaken for a Colonial" (*LM*, 11). Charlie is also one of Blackburn's shy emotional retards, for "He had always preferred engines to girls, and at four-and-twenty he was heartwhole, without the suggestion of a sentimental attachment, past, present or future, to distract his mind from his beloved engineering" (*LM*, 14).

The action of the novel begins on the Vyse family's Natal Sugar Estate, overlooking the Indian Ocean, a plantation which is its own green kingdom of easy wealth and luxurious tropical bungalow culture. This estate is connected to the spa of Durban by the railway line, and to the fashionable circles of London through popular magazines and the latest social novels. The unit of the plantation, however, marooned in its lush landscape, contains an explosive set of social relationships: there is stony Mr. Vyse who has married late, the dominating Mrs. Vyse, newly come into social sway, and her unmarried elder sister, Ella King. Charlie, living as one of the family, and enjoying some esteem as an inventor of a new sugar crusher, is well set to become a sugar baron himself, if he conforms, works hard, and marries well.

But in the very midst of this closed circle is also the paid mother's help, the governess appointed to take care of the Vyse children. Her name is Letty. With his Englishman's lack of discrimination, and lack of a sense of the hierarchy of class on the plantation, Charlie has somewhat unexpectedly fallen, not for the upright, eligible Ella, but for Letty. These are his reasons:

> The average Colonial girl did not appeal to him. He found her [Ella] too regal and vapid—the natural result of conditions in which the men largely outnumber the women and passively concede absolute supremacy to them. Letty was much more interesting. She was by no means well educated from the modern point of view. She had been, she said, to a school in England for three years, where middle-class snobbery and useless knowledge had been instilled in about equal parts. But she had succeeded in absorbing a large amount of useful knowledge, in spite of her teachers, and had read omnivorously, from geometry and political economy to the latest problem novel . . . and to the mentality of the Western woman she added a strange sensuous orientalism. (*LM*, 16–17)

Letty, it soon becomes apparent, is a pale half-caste. Her innate allure, her ability to dress up like her white employers, her passionate ambition to find status for herself in a rigidly apart white world—these are the driving forces that move Letty. Her weak-kneed victim is Charlie, and the entire action of the novel covers his vacillation between doing the right thing by Ella, and being grabbed from her by Letty. Charlie is attracted—insofar as he is anything positive—by Letty's wiles, rather than repelled by her color; for him, the racial taboos simply do not seem to operate.

This triangular tug of war, then, predictably and effectively, by a process of procrastination, builds up to ever more dangerous proportions, until the Charlie affair threatens to rive the sugar clan from top to bottom. The "problem" of color, kept at bay by a number of social controls—the club life, all-white management committees—intrudes into their isolation in the form of Letty. Her attempt to lay hold of an innocent white fellow generates a contest which, step by step, leads to a colonial emergency.

Love Muti is the only Blackburn novel to explore a situation such as this, and to explore it in relatively static terms. The Ella–Charlie–Letty triangle persists for a number of months. For very lengthy sections, Blackburn builds up one arm of the conflict, in an unruffled way, and then, with an equal easiness, moves Charlie into the other arm of the conflict. In *Love Muti* Blackburn creates a more in-depth study than had been his habit before, to such an extent that much of *Love Muti* seems to be by an author transformed. The long gap in time between the writing of *Leaven* and of *Love Muti* might account for this, but the Ella–Charlie–Letty story is, in fact, a different type of tale from any he had previously attempted.

As a result, Letty, Charlie and Ella are characterized with great individuation. Ella emerges as a woman of pride and hauteur, but also one trapped in a social dilemma—marriage is her only way to achieve social independence from her family. While loving Charlie, she also maintains an efficient interest in the local magistrate's assistant, a man whom she betrays when there is a chance of saving Charlie when he is in difficulties with Letty. Charlie, although handled critically, undergoes quiet, understated extremes of suffering in his impotence to resolve his dilemma with any will of his own. Letty, in turn, with all her attraction for fripperies, her coquettishness, her grand gestures on entering society, her miscalculations, and her resort to desperate, melodramatic measures to acquire Charlie, is no mere scheming siren, but a thoroughly understandable person. Never before had Blackburn written so intensely into characters' lives.

The core of the "problem" of *Love Muti* is not merely color; it is the vagaries and mixed motives of love. The fury of the novel is the contest of the two women—Ella the upright is revealed to be tenacious, vital, and even vituperatively jealous; Letty the sultry vamp is shown also to be vulnerable, unsure, and terribly moved by the blaze of her affection. The deadlock between them, conducted in secret notes, or chance meetings at unlikely places, or through the medium of the hapless Charlie, is keyed at a pitch of intensity that, in a way, is not a "color" matter at all. Blackburn's insight into the feminine motivations of two competing individuals in a passionless, cut-and-dried society, where beneath the surface spite, lust, and possessiveness are the ruling powers, is altogether striking and original. Blackburn, who had never before analyzed a woman's temperament to any extent, and then only in passing, seems to have allowed himself this last, slow-moving luxury—a descent into identity—with careful attention to the roles into which colonial society pressed voteless womenkind. The taint of color, which so hamstrings Letty in her social rise, Blackburn sees in *Love Muti* as merely a part of a larger question—the rights of women in general to selfhood.

In *Love Muti* what is so fresh about the handling of the miscegenation theme is that it is Letty, and not Ella, who wins in the end. Once the rumor is out that the respectable Charlie has been seen on occasions with a woman of color in the highspots of Durban—in the plush hotel lobbies with their potted palms, at the theater in a box—Ella is forced either to defend Charlie or to break with him, to live through the opprobrium or to give him up as a lost cause. Ella tenaciously holds on. One of the best orchestrated scenes is at a tennis party where she steps before Charlie and flatly denies the rumor, the rumor which is all too true. Under cover of darkness, however, she meets Letty and, woman to woman, assists her escape from Natal once the police are on to her for her connections with the witch doctors and shady traders involved in the Native Rising. Ella, in short, will act her better and true self at night, in order to maintain the sham of colonial honor and uprightness by daylight.

But Ella loses. Charlie, disgraced by the scandal and dismissed from the Vyse Estate for an inept handling of a patent that could have revolutionized the sugar crushing business, reencounters Letty in the wastes of Zululand, and his enchantment begins. The "love muti" of the title—a charm or medicine—is the so-called witchcraft, or magic, which Letty has access to, in the form of pills, near lethal potions and powders. But those are merely the outward and visible tokens of inward states—Letty herself is a dauntless figure, whose tantalizing wiles, and whose will to power, are intoxicating enough. In a near sadistic way, Letty can conjure with, hypnotize, and break young Charlie and, indeed, for lengthy passages she holds him a limp, listless hostage, a man overpowered by his own unchanneled and blocked desires. Although Blackburn avoids the coy circumlocutions of the time, and the pregnant sexual symbolism of the romancers, his novel is nevertheless very "adult" on erotic issues, or at least adult on the effects of frustrated eroticism.

In *Love Muti* the landscape carries the overpowering sensuality. In lavish descriptions of moonlit beaches, where Letty and Charlie gallop over the glistening tides and past silver lagoons, in the undulating hillsides of sugar cane, in the rocky caves of the northern Natal Drakensberg mountains, Blackburn conveys a rich earthiness against which his characters seem rather puny, tormented creatures. D. H. Lawrence's use of landscape comes to mind here, and Blackburn's novel does look forward to the greater explicitness of the novel after World War I, rather than backward to his dry satires and bachelorly adventures. In *Love Muti* the novel travels ever inward, too, rather than outwards toward new geographical frontiers, and this inward movement signals the birth of psychological realism in South African fiction.

As a portrait of Natal Colony between the war and Union, *Love Muti* is a unique work. Partly, we might feel, Blackburn was responding to the new wave of psychological writing that was coming into vogue in London during the period. With the Empire's expansionist phase finally over, the turning of the frontier inward to study the personality and the norms of the now settled community was inevitable, though. In *Love Muti* it seems as if the basic dispensation under which the characters live has changed, and this new circumstance has caused the change in the nature of the novel.

The Natal of Blackburn's *Love Muti* is highly organized, cunningly held together by the secret service, by law and order, and by efficient transportation networks. It is also a society held in check by magistrates and prisons, and where the telephone and the telegraph can summon up military intervention with a few hours' notice. All this apparatus of the modern state is in full control in *Love Muti*. So distant seem the days of Blackburn's previous freebooting world that we cannot help noticing how hard he struggles to find a pocket of uncolonized land for his climactic scenes in the wilds—Letty and Charlie trek, literally, for days to get away from civilization, and are discovered in their retreat within hours. The new Natal, in *Love Muti,* is no longer the playground it was for the adventure novel. Letty's ally, the old tribal witch doctor, who schemes to drive the white man into the sea with a Maxim gun, is dead by the end of the action, and so is his resisting spirit.

Letty's story, then, is a story of necessary upward mobility in a world in which there is no longer much possibility of escape. While Charlie is temporarily lost to Ella, in the middle of the action, Letty sides with an interesting Blackburn character, one Sam Croxted, a white trader who has lived beyond the pale of white society for many years and taken several black wives, giving rise to several families by them. Croxted falls for Letty, but Natal proves too small for them, too parochial and too conventional. It is to the new Transvaal that they escape. In the cosmopolitan society of Johannesburg they neither of them experience any disadvantage due to a past.

Postwar Johannesburg, in Blackburn's eyes, offered a clean slate to any man with business enterprise, and to any woman with the talent and the confidence to hold her own. One of the satirical delights of *Love Muti* is how the dusty metropolis, still money-grubbing and commercial to be sure, now is an open society which offers more freedom to the renegade and the social misfit than any other quarter of the globe. In Johannesburg Sam Croxted and Letty Bandusa flourish, and it is to Johannesburg that Charlie, too, ventures in the end, to give himself over to Letty. As the novel draws to a conclusion, Charlie for once has his hands near riches as well, and with Letty on his arm is set to make a killing in South Africa's first large-scale, polyglot urban complex. The impulse toward rebellion, the fury of revolt, Blackburn implies, may be rechanneled into the system if the color bar is dispensed with, and a free-for-all is allowed to ensue within the larger economic system. That is what Blackburn meant by the South African "renaissance." So, in *Love Muti*, the feudal plantation estate system proves threatened from within by its own oppressed serfs, and the metropolitan, democratic, color-free complex is posited as an alternative system in which men and women may compete for themselves as best they can, and come into their own.

The end of *Love Muti,* with its vision of a harmonious and productive golden land of opportunity, in which differences of color, gender, and of class are subsumed within a greater whole, for a greater common good, is the fitting, and touching, point at which Blackburn ends his career as a novelist. The struggle of interpersonal relationships in *Love Muti,* Blackburn implies, is worth it, for the wrangle itself produces the new personalities who could remodel South Africa. *Love Muti* asserts that Letty, with her rouged cheeks, her wild-cat smile, her dark burbling laugh, her mastery of English custom, and her African heart, can survive and even prosper in a society which can combine backgrounds as disparate as hers.

Unfortunately, history and Blackburn part company at this point, for the Act of Union which was being debated while Blackburn was writing *Love Muti* was to take anything but such an inclusive view of the nature of South African society and its potential. Letty and her kind were, after 1910, to be excluded from the franchise, even in areas like the Cape where her "coloured" male cousins had enjoyed the vote. In the 1920s the Immorality Act, which had been an unwritten custom of the colonies, would become written law, too, and interracial marriages like Letty and Charlie's declared illegal. Blackburn's vision of the South African future—the only vision he could foresee as resulting in prosperity and racial harmony—was to be profoundly thwarted in practice. Once again, we have found a good reason why Blackburn's commentary has not found favor. The South Africa he hoped for proved unimaginable to his readers. And today, sixty years on, it is even hard to believe that he thought Letty would win, when it is Ella King who continues to rule.

But the poignancy of Letty's last speech, before her eventual engagement to Charlie, remains. It reads like the impassioned plea of South Africa herself to the better side of her rulers:

You can never understand—you are English. You have never been anything but what you are, and cannot comprehend what it must mean for a refined and educated woman like me to suffer the degradation of being despised as an inferior by white women who can scarcely read, who were reared as scullery-maids, but being pure-blooded can lord it over me. And then to go through life knowing that every white man regards you as a fit subject for any insult. That is what I have had to bear until you came into my life and gave me the courage to uphold my womanhood and feel that one good white man sympathised with and supported me. Can you wonder that I love you. . . . (*LM*, 344)

It is out of lone acts of courage—like the uncommitted Charlie's, when he accepts Letty's proposal—that true unions are made. Blackburn, the real drifting Englishman of this study, symbolically at any rate, also accepted the love of the mixed, tainted land that gave him his being as a writer.

That acceptance, at the end of his career, was also, as it happens, his farewell. But in *Love Muti* he left behind some potent symbols. A notable one is the symbol of the caterpillar and the tennis racket, with which *Love Muti* opens and closes:

[Letty] was busy heading off a huge caterpillar at her feet, using the head of her racket to block the progress of the creature. . . .

"Don't you see? This thing knows there is something stopping him, but never having met a racket before, he can't understand why he doesn't get on. If he did, he would pass through the network. But perhaps he doesn't want to pass through." (*LM*, 12)

While she and Charlie natter idly on, he commenting on her talking in code, she commenting on his unimaginativeness, the action is diverted. But at the end of the scene:

The man was watching and admiring the woman; she, perfectly conscious of the fact, was affecting not to know it. Suddenly:
"There! The beastie has discovered the secret and has got through."
She held up the racket. The caterpillar had passed through the network and was exploring the other side. She placed it gently on the grass.
"Go on, you have won," she said, addressing the insect.
"I suppose there is some sort of a moral hanging on to that, but I was never good at guessing riddles. . . ." (*LM*, 12–13)

For the reader, the moral is plain. *Love Muti* is its fine illustration.

Chapter Five
Conclusion

The life and work of Douglas Blackburn poses a singular problem to researchers and students alike. During the course of this book we have come across abundant evidence that his story is an anomalous one, worthy of one of his own plots. It is truly ironic that the man who witnessed such a cross-section of South African history, who ranged so extensively behind the scenes, and who was driven by a sense of his times vanishing into the past, should in turn have been overlooked by historians of South African literature. With Blackburn rediscovered, so is an epoch of tumultuous changes and formative events. And with that rediscovery, the literary history of South Africa has to be modified.

The truth about Blackburn's status and position in the chronology of South African writing is that, at the present time, he is a missing figure. His name is hardly a household word, and all but one of his works remain out of print. So forgotten is the once-renowned Blackburn that during the course of conducting the research for this book I often felt I was wrestling with a shadow. So despondent did I become at times, especially when asked what I was working on, that I would dodge the question and reply that I was just reevaluating Olive Schreiner, of course. Yet the sense that unknown Blackburn was, and still is, a figure worth detailed and serious attention kept me going. I need never have doubted his existence, even if the strange case of his identity, and the even stranger case of his persona as a writer, has proved hard to crack.

To put none too fine a literary-critical point to it, I feel that Blackburn is missing for a rather simple and wretched reason. There has been prevalent in the British colonies a notion, which I believe is a distorted version of a European notion, that literature is, or should be, somehow above the hurly-burly of daily affairs. Literature, so the prejudice goes, should be timeless and universal. A sign of its greatness, this reasoning continues, is its detachment from current affairs, its applicability to all situations at all times at some abstract, even sublime level. Given this criteria of Olympian aloofness, it is not surprising that to the purist and the absolutist the whole field of South African literature has apparently yielded very few works that could be said to pass muster. Schreiner's *The Story of an African Farm* generally qualifies, precisely on the grounds of its tendency to philosophize and abstract from African experience in a European way. To this day, university departments of English in South Africa hesitate to study South African work. The results in the historiography of South African literature have been grievously prejudicial to the "local" author, and have retarded research into the literature for several generations. And when the South African author does come into his own in literary research, Blackburn is doubly penalized, for he was actually a British writer.

The bad news for the universalizers, however, is that almost all of South African literature in English has always been rooted in quotidian events, and in a singular fashion. The commentary that Schreiner's *African Farm* makes on the universal verities is equally strongly matched by the commentary she makes on urgent matters of her day, like the colonizing impulse, the vulnerability of the independent pastoralist, the inapplicability of exported education, the myths of power that shape the frontier world, not to mention the "woman question," for which she is probably most warmly remembered. The actuality of South African literature in English is that it has always waged poetry, fiction, and drama as if they were pitched battle, and the impulse to assess political and social issues through writing has always proved the source of its vitality.

Rather than ignoring Blackburn, then, on the grounds that he was too deeply involved with the burning issues of his own times, the question to ask about him should now perhaps be stood on its head: how successfully did Blackburn confront and draw inspiration from the issues of his day, and how successfully was he able to work through those issues in the artifacts of his fiction? These, at least, are preferable approaches to pursue than the arrogant and ignorant approaches that are more usual: who was Douglas Blackburn, followed by what was the Z.A.R., what was Natal Colony, was there a Raid, a War, a Rebellion, and is it important to remember them?— or the most galling of all—did anything happen between Schreiner in the 1880s and Pauline Smith in the 1920s?

The problem the Blackburn case poses is thus a major one. To solve it in full would require a scope larger than that of this book. Blackburn was part of a currently neglected tradition of Victorian and Edwardian writing that, once it spun off into overseas territories, took on rich and rewarding manifestations. He belonged to the tradition of the journalist-novelist who used fiction as the next step away from daily reporting to give timely and fully detailed reports of an overseas society hardly known to the smug homeland of literary Britain. Rudyard Kipling was the founder of this school in British literary history. Perceval Gibbon, W. C. Scully, Stephen Black, and Herman Charles Bosman—Blackburn's contemporaries and juniors, who all held him in awesome respect—were also followers of Kipling. Like Kipling, Blackburn always maintained a strong link with the "news of the day," whether actually as a man of the press out on assignment, or as an editorializer whose fictional output was integrally related to that information-bearing function. Such was the power and scope of the press of the turn of the century, that a fair and intelligent living could be made out of it. In South African literature, much of the work of the high colonial period (say, from 1880 to 1914) is, in fact, of this type, so that if we tend to undervalue it we are casually denying the possibility of there having been any literature at all during this hectic period.

But it is when a writer, formed by existing circumstances of his day, rises out of those circumstances with some kind of glory that the critic should take especial note. I have argued here in detail as to the value and the skill of Blackburn's artistry as a writer of those days, and shown with regard to his novels that there is a detailed case to be made for his extraordinary abilities and unique accomplishments in the South African novel. In the mainstream British novel, beyond that, there may well be no room to elbow him in for a spot of repute.

But in terms of the development of, and the interest of, South African fiction, his role is of crucial importance to the whole. With Blackburn we can begin to redefine its nature, and with Blackburn we can also enjoy the comic invention, the astute commentary, and the superb intelligence of his wonderful career.

There was no one like him, and to lose him once more would be to lose a world that was magnificently his.

Notes and References

Chapter One

1. *The Anglo-African Who's Who,* ed. Walter H. Wills and R. J. Barrett (London: Routledge and Sons, 1905).
2. Walter H. Wills, ed. (London: L. Upcott Gill; Johannesburg: Juta and Co., 1907).
3. See Eric Rosenthal, comp., *The South African Dictionary of National Biography* (London: Frederick Warne, 1966), and A. C. Partridge, in *The Standard Encyclopedia of South Africa* (Cape Town: Nasou, 1972).
4. See Rupert Croft-Cooke, "Douglas Blackburn," in *The Altar in the Loft* (London, 1960), pp. 124–31; see also his *The Glittering Pastures* (London, 1962), p. 109.
5. See *Kruger's Secret Service* (London, 1900), pp. 160–61.
6. Interview with Rupert Croft-Cooke, Bournemouth, June 30, 1975.
7. Anonymous interview, Tonbridge, June 28, 1979.
8. Ibid.
9. H. R. Pratt Boorman and Eric Maskell, *Tonbridge Free Press Centenary* (Tonbridge: Tonbridge Free Press, 1969), p. 28.
10. Interview by telephone with Eric Maskell, Tonbridge, July 13, 1976.
11. *Thought-reading, or Modern Mysteries Explained* (London, 1884), p. 7; hereafter cited in the text as *TR*.
12. After a reputable career as a secretary to the Society for Psychical Research, Smith went into show business, and later invented color moving pictures, for which he was much honored before his death at the age of ninety-five in 1959.
13. *Brightonian* (Brighton), November 12, 1881.
14. "Confessions of a Famous Medium—1," *John Bull* (London), December 5, 1908, p. 590.
15. "Confessions of a Famous Medium—4," *John Bull,* December 26, 1908, p. 706.
16. For example: "Mr Douglas Blackburn, expert in hand-writing, who has studied the subject for twenty-five years, and has given expert evidence forty-four times, said that he had carefully examined the samples of handwriting submitted to him, and was emphatically of the opinion that all the writings in the letters signed 'J. Anthony Roos' except one, were

written by the same person who wrote the cheque . . ." ("Who Wrote the Letters," *Bloemfontein Post* [Bloemfontein] (December 12, 1902).

17. Trevor H. Hall, *The Strange Case of Edmund Gurney* (London, 1964).

18. First televized in the Theater 625 series on October 29, 1967.

19. This detail recurs in Blackburn. For example: "The visitor to St. Paul's Cathedral, London, cannot fail to be struck by the almost complete monopoly enjoyed by successful soldiers and sailors in the monumental department. You may look long and vainly for a monument to some apostle of peace who benefited the world by manufacture or industry; the temple of the Prince of Peace has no room for these. It is successful wholesale butchers whose memorials are alone deemed worth recording" (*Transvaal Sentinel*, February 13, 1897). Being a butcher's son turned vegetarian, Blackburn was sensitive on the subject of carnage, and consistently maintained a pacifist line.

20. Trevor H. Hall was the first to trace Blackburn's details of birth.

21. In the *Brightonian* it is particularly clear that Blackburn felt strongly about civic hygiene. Vol. 6 includes a cartoon envisioning an electrified Brighton, with parks open to the people. To the local Sanitary Congress he recommends: "No More Private Slaughterhouses!"

22. Manfred Nathan, *Not Heaven Itself: An Autobiography* (Durban, 1944), p. 96.

23. See Manfred Nathan, *South African Literature* (Cape Town, 1925).

24. Editorial, *Brightonian*, October 22, 1880, under the slogan "An Independent Weekly Journal and Critical Review of Local Topics."

25. See Stephen Gray, "Douglas Blackburn: Journalist into Novelist," *English in Africa* (Grahamstown) 5, no. 1 (March 1978). This number includes a selection of pieces by Blackburn from the two *Sentinels*, pp. 8–31, and a selection of the Blackburn-Blackwood letters, pp. 34–45.

26. Editorial, *Sentinel* (Krugersdorp) 1, no. 3 (April 1, 1896).

27. Ibid. The *Sentinel* hereafter cited in the text as *S*, and the *Transvaal Sentinel* as *TS*.

28. See "Chivalry: A Lady Called a Liar—Mr Blackburn Again," *Standard and Diggers' News* (Johannesburg), May 24, 1897.

29. See William Hills, "Douglas Blackburn: Some Personal Recollections," *Star* (Johannesburg), April 3, 1929.

30. From March 25 to April 13, 1897.

31. *Tonbridge Free Press*, February 22, 1918; hereafter cited in the text as *TFP*.

32. *Secret Service in South Africa* (London, 1911), p. 237.

33. *The Krugersdorp Standard* (Krugersdorp), April 8, 1899.

34. Ibid., December 24, 1898.

35. In the Strange Collection, Johannesburg Public Library. Like the *Moon, Life* is not listed in *The Union List of South African Newspapers* (Cape Town: South African Public Library, 1950).
36. *Life: A Sub-tropical Journal,* March 4, 1899.
37. "The Preliminary Causes [War Number]," *Times of Natal* (Pietermaritzburg), October 1900, unpaged.
38. "Blackburn-Blackwood Letters," *English in Africa,* p. 35; hereafter cited in the text as *EiA*.
39. See M. van Wyk Smith, *Drummer Hodge: The Poetry of the Anglo-Boer War* (Oxford: Clarendon Press, 1978).
40. Donald J. Weinstock, in "The Two Boer Wars and the Jameson Raid: A Checklist of Novels in English," *Research in African Literatures* (Austin, Texas) 3, no. 1 (Spring 1972), lists over 200.
41. W. W. Caddell to Mr. H. R. Lakeman, May 9, 1929, in the National English Literary Museum, Grahamstown.
42. "The Marvels of Loteni: A Voice from the Dead," *Natal Witness* (Pietermaritzburg), June 19, 1902.
43. Hills, see note 29 above.
44. *The Prince,* however, plays a crucial role in the action of *Love Muti*.
45. Foreword to *Secret Service in South Africa,* p. iii.
46. Interview with Rupert Croft-Cooke.
47. *Daily Mail* (London), June 24, 1915.
48. Original in my possession.
49. Rowland Ryder, *Edith Cavell* (London: Hamish Hamilton, 1975), p. 214.

Chapter Two

1. *Kruger's Secret Service* (London, 1900), pp. 197–98; hereafter cited in the text as *KSS*.
2. Mark Twain, *More Tramps Abroad* (also known as *Following the Equator*) (London: Chatto and Windus, 1898), p. 467.
3. This section of *KSS* is a fictional embodiment of views expressed by Blackburn and Manfred Nathan in their anonymous pamphlet of January 1896, "The Revolution—and After: Being the Secret History of a Failure." Any doubts about the authorship of the former may be dispelled by comparing it with the latter. For a contrasting view, see the anonymous pamphlet which answered Blackburn and Nathan, "A Complete Vindication of the Reform Movement" (Johannesburg: February 1896). Also, presumably at Blackburn's suggestion, Ben J. Viljoen entered this war of the pamphleteers after the Jameson Raid by writing "myne eerste poging om 'n boekie op te stellen" with his 28-page "Die Rebellie van 1895–96 in de Z. Afrikaansche Republiek," printed by *Ons Volk* in Krugersdorp.

4. Some twenty years earlier, when Blackburn's *Brightonian* was broken by the Munster case, involving his defamation of the Brighton town councillor, the crucial issue was Blackburn's championship of two petty thieves who had been paid to rob Munster of certain incriminating papers. The graphic scene of the burglary in *KSS* is analogous.

5. Blackburn seems never to have visited the Robben Island leper colony. In Krugersdorp, however, one of his close friends was Dr. Max Mehliss, who had ridden with Ben Viljoen's commando against Jameson. The famous "Dr. Mealies" ran a leper colony, and was the patron of rehabilitating jailbirds. Blackburn acted as best man at Mehliss' wedding (*S*, September 9, 1896) and frequently praised his practical tackling of social problems. Like Blackburn, Mehliss eschewed ostentation, and was given a pauper's burial.

6. See the letters column of the *Spectator* (London), December 13, 1902, pp. 938-39, where Blackburn lured Haggard into some fatuous comments on the subject of "Kaffir telegraphy" (on December 27, p. 1026).

7. Literary legend has it that Haggard himself raised the flag in Pretoria's Church Square in April 1877 to symbolize the British Crown's annexation of the Transvaal.

8. *Richard Hartley, Prospector* (Edinburgh, 1905), pp. 3-4; hereafter cited in the text as *RHP*.

9. See *Secret Service in South Africa*, p. 322: "James Couper, who combined literary tastes with successful pugilism, wrote a book which, under the title of *Mixed Humanity*, gave the best, in fact the only large and full, description of life in Kimberley in its early days."

10. Bulalie (Billali) is the shaman in *She*, and the Bulalie of *RHP* recurs as the main character of *Leaven*. In Zulu the name means "killer."

11. Unsigned review of *RHP*, *Star* (Johannesburg), November 28, 1905.

Chapter Three

1. *Prinsloo of Prinsloosdorp* (London, 1899), p. 1; hereafter cited in the text as *PP*. Page numbers in subsequent editions vary by no more than two or three.

2. *Spectator* (London), August 26, 1899, p. 288.

3. Stanley Portal Hyatt, review of *Secret Service in South Africa*, *Bookman* (London), October 1911, pp. 53-54.

4. Jack Cope, "Satire and Humour in South African Verse," in *Poetry South Africa*, ed. Peter Wilhelm and James A. Polley (Johannesburg, 1976), p. 61.

5. Quoted in A. St. John Adcock, "The Literature of Greater Britain," *Bookman*, September 1912, p. 248.

6. S. G. Liebson, "The South Africa of Fiction," *State* (Cape Town), February 1912, p. 137.
7. In *African Monthly* (Grahamstown) 1, no. 1.
8. See "Mulder's Drift 1898," *Daily Dispatch* (East London), January 20, 1979.
9. "Masterly Satire of Old Transvaal," *Eastern Province Herald* (Port Elizabeth), December 19, 1978.
10. "Prinsloosgate Revisited," *Sunday Times* (Johannesburg), December 17, 1978.
11. "New South African Writing, 1978–79," *Standpunte* (Cape Town) 34, no. 4 (August 1981):26.
12. *A Burgher Quixote* (Edinburgh, 1903), p. 331; hereafter cited in the text as *BQ*.
13. Musings without Method column, *Blackwood's Magazine* (Edinburgh), June 1903, pp. 855–56.
14. Unsigned review of *BQ*, *Natal Witness* (Pietermaritzburg), July 4, 1903.
15. See Ben J. Viljoen, *Under the Vierkleur: A Romance of a Lost Cause* (Boston: Small, Maynard and Co., 1904) (also published in Dutch translation in Amsterdam in the same year as *Danie*): "the story is based on and its scenes are drawn from actual episodes of the late war in South Africa.... I have tried to present my characters as truly and as characteristically as I could, without bearing too much either on their follies or their heroisms, the innate gentleness and simplicity of heart of their prototypes, or their general lack of those refinements of modern culture which the wide establishment of schools and systems of higher education alone can supply. For I come of a simple people, and as such I have tried to describe them.... That I wrote it in English, instead of having it translated from my mother tongue, was solely for the fear of losing by translation some of my real meaning" (pp. viii, x). The prewar Blackburn-Viljoen friendship must have been the start of the inspiration for the Sarel Erasmus sequence. Ironically, when the war came, Blackburn was at, or even was wounded at, the Battle of Pieter's Hill, at which the Boer forces on the other side were commanded by his disciple, Viljoen.
16. "Some South African Prejudices," *Chambers's Journal* (London), November 22, 1902, p. 814.
17. *I Came and Saw* (London, 1908), p. xix; hereafter cited in the text as *ICS*.
18. See F. R. Statham, *Mr Magnus* (London: T. Fisher Unwin, 1896).
19. I have traced only two poems by Blackburn, apart from the one quoted earlier from the *Brightonian*. One of these, "The Converted Missionary," first appeared in the *New Age* (London), November 7, 1912, p. 9, and is reprinted in *A Century of South African Poetry*, ed. Michael

Chapman (Johannesburg: Ad. Donker, 1981). It tells the story of Bigsby the missionary, converted by Jack the heathen to savagery. Like Sixpence, Jack turns to show business as the Wild Man from Gogo, and this mocking ballad retells much of the rest of the plot of *ICS* and of *Leaven*. The other poem, "The Church's Favorite Child" (*New Age*, October 12, 1912), is about the failure of the church adequately to educate even its own home parishioners.

20. See, for example, "Transvaal Treasure-hunts," *Chambers's Journal*, September 1906, pp. 661–63, or "In Quest of a Treasure-cave," *Wide World Magazine* (London) 9, no. 23 (1906): 173–81. These deal, among other things, with the myth of the elephants' dying ground, which is central to *Love Muti*.

21. This quintessentially Blackburn comment is the key to his consistent and determined anticlericism.

Chapter Four

1. Rivers's publication list including spring and summer announcements, 1908, bound after the text of *Leaven*, p. 4.

2. This occurs in the same prison where Sarel Erasmus will write his war memoirs, and Letty Bandusa in *Love Muti* will be held for trial on a charge of high treason.

3. *Leaven* (London, 1908), p. 281; hereafter cited in the text as *L*.

4. See Christine Isabel Hofmeyr, "Mining, Social Change and Literature: An Analysis of South African Literature with Particular Reference to the Mining Novel (1870–1920)" (M.A. thesis, University of the Witwatersrand, Johannesburg, 1980), pp. 96–101.

5. "The Safeguard of Kafir Socialism," *New Age* (London), October 3, 1908, p. 448.

6. "Natal and the Native Question," *Star* (Johannesburg), December 27, 1902.

7. Unsigned review of *L*, quoted on the facing title p. of *ICS*.

8. Unsigned review of *L*, *Bookman* (London) 34, no. 204 (September 1908):231.

9. Unsigned review of *L*, *Academy* (London), July 25, 1908.

10. Unsigned review of *L*, *Daily Mail* (London), August 15, 1908.

11. "The Problem of Black and White: How a Novelist would Treat it: Hysteria from Basutoland," unsigned review of *L*, *Cape Argus Weekly Review* (Cape Town), October 21, 1908, p. 8.

12. William Plomer, *Turbott Wolfe* (Johannesburg: Ad. Donker, 1980), p. 65.

13. Michael Wade, *Peter Abrahams* (London: Evans Bros., 1972), p. 49.

14. *Love Muti* (London, 1915), p. 264; hereafter cited in the text as *LM*. These issues strongly resemble those dealt with in Sol T. Plaatje's *Mhudi*, written in the 1910s.
15. Douglas Blackburn to Mr. Blackwood, Natal Club, Maritzburg, Christmas, 1903; transcript in the National English Literary Museum.

Selected Bibliography

PRIMARY SOURCES

1. Novels

A Burgher Quixote. Edinburgh and London: Wm. Blackwood & Sons, 1903.
I Came and Saw. London: Alston Rivers, 1908.
Kruger's Secret Service, by One Who was in It. London: John Macqueen, 1900.
Leaven: A Black and White Story. London: Alston Rivers, 1908.
Love Muti. London: Everett & Co., 1915.
Prinsloo of Prinsloosdorp: A Tale of Transvaal Officialdom, by Sarel Erasmus. London and Johannesburg: Dunbar Bros., 1899. London: Alston Rivers, 1908. Cape Town: South African Universities Press, 1978.
Richard Hartley, Prospector. Edinburgh and London: Wm. Blackwood & Sons, 1905.

2. Factual Works

The Detection of Forgery: A Practical Handbook. London: Charles & Edwin Layton, 1909. With Captain Waithman Caddell.
The Martyr Nurse: The Death and Achievement of Edith Cavell. London: Ridd Masson, 1915.
Print Shorthand: The Office System. London: Blackdell & Co., 1912.
Secret Service in South Africa. London: Cassell & Co., 1911. With Captain W. Waithman Caddell.
Thought-reading, or Modern Mysteries Explained. London: Field & Tuer, 1884.

3. Selected Articles

"Animal Superstitions." *Man* (London), December 1904, pp. 181–83.
Blackburn issue. *English in Africa* (Grahamstown) 5, no. 1 (March 1978):8–47.
"Confessions of a Famous Medium, 1–6." *John Bull* (London), December 5, 1908–January 9, 1909.
"Ghosts and Mediums I have Met, 1–5." *Tonbridge Free Press* (Tonbridge), February 13–April 5, 1920.
"If There Should be War." *Transvaal Sentinel* (Krugersdorp) 1, no. 33 (June 19, 1897). 6 pp.

"Natal and the Native Question." *Star* (Johannesburg), December 27, 1902.
"Preliminary Causes." *Times of Natal War Number* (Pietermaritzburg), 1900, unpaged.
"Rand Magnate's Latest Plot." *New Age* (London), November 12, 1908, p. 47.
"Some South African Prejudices." *Chambers's Journal* (London), November 22, 1902, pp. 813–15.
"The Marvels of Loteni: A Voice from the Dead." *Natal Witness* (Pietermaritzburg), June 19, 1902.
"The Revolution—and After: Being the Secret History of a Failure." Johannesburg: George Thompson, 1896. 15 pp.
"The Safeguard of Kafir Socialism." *New Age* (London), October 3, 1908, p. 448.
"Transvaal Treasure-hunts." *Chambers's Journal* (London), September 1906, pp. 661–63.
"Treasure Tales." *Daily Mail* (London), April 24, 1923.

SECONDARY SOURCES

Adcock, A. St. J. "The Literature of Greater Britain." *Bookman* (London), September 1912, pp. 247–50. A survey of South African writing up to the time, with the emphasis on topical colonial issues.
Anon. "A New South African Satirist." *Spectator* (London) 3, no. 713 (August 26, 1899):288–90. An early descriptive review of *Prinsloo of Prinsloosdorp,* perceptive and appreciative, which launched Blackburn on his career as a serious creative writer.
Chapman, M., ed. *A Century of South African Poetry.* Johannesburg: Ad. Donker, 1981. Includes Blackburn's longest poem, and argues the case for an alternative tradition in South African literature to which a radical like Blackburn belongs.
Cope, J. "Satire and Humour in South African Verse." In *Poetry South Africa,* edited by Peter Wilhelm and James A. Polley. Johannesburg: Ad. Donker, 1976. A survey of some satire in verse that specifically excludes Blackburn from the liberal-tempered tradition in South Africa.
Croft-Cooke, R. *The Altar in the Loft.* London: Putnam, 1960. A memoir which includes a chapter on several meetings with Blackburn and on his impressive raconteurism in Kentish village life.
———. *The Glittering Pastures.* London: Putnam, 1962. Describes Blackburn's fascination with, and respect for, Rudyard Kipling.
Gray, S. "Douglas Blackburn: Journalist into Novelist (1857–1929)." *English in Africa* (Grahamstown) 5, no. 1 (March 1978):1–7. An

introduction to Blackburn's career as a reporter, particularly in the 1890s, preceding a selection of his articles.

———. "Douglas Blackburn: Unknown Writer, Unknown Work." *Unisa English Studies* (Pretoria) 14, nos. 2–3 (September 1976):44–51. A survey of Blackburn's life and work, and the reasons why he is excluded from traditional South African reading syllabuses.

———. "Piet's Progress: Douglas Blackburn's Satire on the Foundation of the Transvaal." *English Studies in Africa* (Johannesburg) 24, no. 1 (March 1981):25–36. An account of the background and context of *Prinsloo of Prinsloosdorp*.

Hall, T. R. *The Strange Case of Edmund Gurney*. London: Duckworth, 1964. An expose of fake mediums and psychic tricksters which includes the first correct description of Blackburn's early career.

Hills, W. "Douglas Blackburn: Some Personal Recollections." *Star* (Johannesburg), April 3, 1929. The fullest obituary of Blackburn by a South African journalist who knew him in Krugersdorp and Pietermaritzburg.

Hyatt, S. P. "Secret Service and Open Vices." *Bookman* (London) 41. no. 241 (October 1911):53–54. A fellow novelist's review-article on *Secret Service in South Africa*, putting Blackburn's co-history into perspective.

Liebson, S. G. "The South Africa of Fiction." *State* (Cape Town), February 1912, pp. 135–39. A survey of the South African novel, which with good insight situates Blackburn in the context of colonial satire. As Sarah Gertrude Millin, this author would later become typical of the "racial" school of novelists.

Nagelgast, E. B. "Johannesburg Newspapers and Periodicals, 1887–1899." In *Africana Byways*, edited by Anna H. Smith. Johannesburg: Ad. Donker, 1976, pp. 89–113. A detailed survey of the formative period of the English-language press in the Transvaal.

Nathan, M. *Not Heaven Itself*. Durban: Knox, 1944. An autobiography by an acquaintance of Blackburn's from his days on Johannesburg's *Star* newspaper.

———. *South African Literature: A General Survey*. Cape Town: Juta, 1925. An uncritical but inclusive survey of the writing in South Africa of all genres, creative and factual, which accords Blackburn fair space.

Index

Academy, The (London), 128
Alston Rivers, Ltd., 34, 74, 78, 109, 112, 125, 127
Anglo-Boer War. *See* South African War

Bain, Andrew Geddes, 16
Bambata Rebellion, 132, 134
Bennett, Arnold, 3
Black, Stephen, 131, 144
Blackburn, Charles (spiritualist), 6
Blackburn, Douglas. Birth, 1–2, 12; Brighton period, 4, 8–10, 109; cryptologist, 10, 42, 145n16; death, 2, 4–5, 31, 38; Johannesburg periods, 11, 13–15, 19, 22–23, 25–27, 33, 45–46, 53, 60, 63, 65, 73–74, 139; Krugersdorp period, 4, 13, 18–24, 28, 32, 53, 57, 74; libel cases, 1, 8, 148n14; London periods, 10–12, 34–35, 42, 52, 101–102, 104–107, 109, 132; Loteni Valley period, 1, 30–32, 34, 40, 61, 93, 112, 121; Pietermaritzburg period, 4, 28, 31, 33, 113–14, 122, 126; Tonbridge period, 4–6, 35, 38, 128

WORKS: FACTUAL
Angelo; or An Ideal Love, 8
"Beginnings and Development of Deep-level Mining at Witwatersrand", 17
Detection of Forgery, The, 35
Disenchantment, 8
"If There Should be War", 22
Martyr Nurse, The, 37
Print Shorthand: The Office System, 37
"Revolution–and After: Being the Secret History of a Failure", 147n3
Secret Service in South Africa, 36–37, 72, 76, 94
Thought-reading, or Modern Mysteries Explained, 6–7

WORKS: NOVELS
Burgher Quixote, A, 1, 3, 28, 32–34, 41, 66, 73, 77–96, 109, 112
I Came and Saw, 32, 34, 66, 96–110, 112, 118, 120
Kruger's Secret Service, 18, 40–52, 59, 65, 72–73, 84
Leaven: A Black and White Story, 1, 32, 34, 64, 91, 94, 106, 109, 112–31, 134, 136
Love Muti, 33, 35, 94, 112, 124, 131–41
Prinsloo of Prinsloosdorp, 1–2, 32, 34, 40–42, 49, 65–78, 81, 84, 86, 109, 113
Richard Hartley, Prospector, 1, 32, 34, 40–41, 52–65, 73, 77, 93–95, 120, 126, 134
Study in Anarchy, A, 108–109, 112

Blackburn, George (sailor), 3
Blackwood's, Edinburgh, 28, 32–

34, 56, 58, 74, 78, 108–109, 133
Blackwood's Magazine (Edinburgh), 55, 85
Blake, William, 11
Boksburg Herald, The, 21
Bookman, The (London), 127
Bosman, Herman Charles, 78, 144
Brighton Figaro, The, 10
Brightonian, The, 2, 8–10, 16, 146n21, 148n4
Brownlee, Frank, 114
Buchan, John, 133–34
Bunyan, John, 85

Caddell, W. Waithman, 30, 35–36
Cape Argus Weekly Review (Cape Town), 150n11
Cavell, Edith, 37–38
Cervantes, Miguel de, 45, 73, 84–85, 90
Chambers's Journal (London), 91, 109
Chapman, Michael, 149n19
Christie, Sarah, 78
Churchill, Winston S., 29, 82
City News, The (Manchester), 127
Coleridge, Samuel Taylor, 62
Conrad, Joseph, 4, 34, 133
Cope, Jack, 77
Couper, J. R., 64, 148n9
Crawford, F. Marion, 7
Croft-Cooke, Rupert, 2–4, 38

Daily Mail, The (London), 11, 29, 128–29
Dickens, Charles, 11
Dinizulu, Chief, 132
Doyle, A. Conan, 29, 35
Dunbar Bros., 34, 74
du Plessis, W. P., 78

Erasmus of Rotterdam, 90–91, 100
Everett & Co., 35, 132

Forrest, John, 77
Forster, E. M., 3
Fugard, Athol, 119

Gibbon, Perceval, 33, 131, 144
Gilbert, W. S., 8
Grogan, John, 78
Gurney, Edmund, 9

Haggard, H. Rider, 55–60, 64, 71, 120, 125, 148n6, 148n7
Hall, Trevor H., 10
Hardy, Thomas, 133
Hills, William, 33
Hofmeyr, Isabel, 123
Hyatt, Stanley Portal, 75, 77, 148n3

James, Henry, 4
Jameson Raid, 18, 22, 25, 41–46, 52, 61, 64, 71, 143
John Macqueen & Co., 40
Joubert, Piet, 71, 80–81, 83, 91

Kani, John, 119
Kipling, Rudyard, 3–4, 29, 133, 144, 153
Knight, W. S. M., 37
Kruger, President Paul, 13, 17–18, 23, 26–27, 29, 43–44, 47–49, 53, 64, 72, 74–76, 82, 92, 96
Krugersdorp Standard, The, 25

Lawrence, D. H., 3, 138
Life: A Sub-tropical Journal (Johannesburg), 25–26
Livingstone, David, 48
Lytton, Lord, 7

Index

Macnab, William Ramsay, 18, 53
Magato, Chief, 15, 53, 71
Malaboch, Chief, 17
Maskell, Eric, 5–6
Mehliss, Dr Max, 148n5
Mendelssohn, Sidney, 76
Millin, Sarah Gertrude, 77, 154
Milner, Sir Alfred, 27
Moon, The (Johannesburg), 16–18, 147n35

Natal Witness, The (Pietermaritzburg), 86
Nathan, Manfred, 15–17, 147n3
New Age, The (London), 123, 149n19
Ntshona, Winston, 119

Owen, Ken, 78

Partridge, A. C., 145n3
Paton, Alan, 125
Plaatje, Sol T., 151n14
Plomer, William, 130–31
Prince, The (Durban), 33, 147n44
Pringle, Thomas, 16

Radcliffe, Mrs, 7
Raleigh, Sir Walter, 85
Rhodes, Cecil, 14, 17, 22, 44, 48–49, 76, 99
Ridd Masson Co., 37
Ridge, Stanley, 78
Robinson Crusoe (Defoe), 62
Rosenthal, Eric, 145n3

Sammons, William Layton, 16
Schreiner, Olive, 3, 22, 65, 73, 89–90, 142–43
Scully, W. C., 144
Sentinel, The, and *Transvaal Sentinel*, 1–2, 18–25, 34, 48, 57, 86, 118–19, 146n19

Slocum, Joshua, 3
Smith, George Albert, 7, 9–10, 145n12
Smith, Pauline, 143
Smith, 'Scotty', 75, 81
Society for Psychical Research, 6–7, 145n12
South African War, 3, 11, 14, 27–30, 40–41, 51–52, 55, 63, 79–80, 85, 87–88, 98, 143
Spectator, The (London), 74–75, 148n6
Standard and Diggers' News, The (Johannesburg), 18, 25
Stanley, H. M., 48
Star, The (Johannesburg), 14–18, 21, 26, 65
Statham, F. R., 99
Stead, W. T., 11, 22
Stowe, Harriet Beecher, 127
Sussex Post, The, 8
Swift, Jonathan, 75
Swinburne, A. C., 25

Taylor, Ken, 10
Tennyson, Alfred Lord, 61
Theal, George McCall, 78
Times of Natal, The (Pietermaritzburg), 28–29
Todd, Richard, 10
Tonbridge Free Press, The, 4–6, 30, 38–39
Transvaal Sentinel. See Sentinel
Transvaal Staats Courant (Pretoria), 62
Twain, Mark, 44

van Wyk Smith, M., 147n39
Viljoen, Ben J., 24, 80, 86–87, 147n3, 149n15
Voortrekker, De (Krugersdorp), 18

Wade, Michael, 131
Wallace, Edgar, 11, 29, 51
Weinstock, Donald J., 147n40
Weinthal, Leo, 16
Wells, H. G., 3
Wide World Magazine, The (London), 110

Wild Man from Gogo, 102, 150n19
Wilde, Oscar, 25
Wordsworth, William, 62

Zulu Rebellion. *See* Bambata Rebellion